THE WHITE EARTH
SNOWSHOE GUIDE BOOK

Snowshoe Tracks

Snowshoe tracks lead off
Up the mounded road
Toward the cutting peaks.

Graceful, always gracefully
The lone snowshoe tracks weave for
Like the tracks of the squirrel
The snowshoe tracks belong here.

And in the spring
The snowshoe tracks
Like the tracks of the coyote
Will fall away
Leaving the fresh moss to steam.

By David Ellis
From Bastien Brothers Inc.
Village Huron, Quebec

Thomas Hollatz

THE WHITE EARTH
SNOWSHOE
GUIDE BOOK

NORTH STAR PRESS

Saint Cloud,   Minnesota

Special thanks to: The Drewniak's, Sen. Mike Gravel, Carl Marty, Eugene Radloff, Herman Smith, J. P. Tanguay, C. Vig, The Wilsies and Louis and Virginia Hollatz.

This book is dedicated to those who use winter — not to the bastards who abuse it.

Photographic Credits: Sources for illustrations in this book are as follows: Alaskan Travel Bureau, 59, 61, 62, 71; Associated Press, 47, 94; Bastien Brothers, 5, 16; Black Forest Enterprises, 7; Bureau of Indian Affairs, 70; Cal Green, 8; Cedric Vig, 30; The Chicago Tribune, 96; John N. Dwyer, 33, 34; Paul A. Dwyer, 38, 40, 41, 42, 43, 44; Eugene Radloff, 51, 52, 64, 99; Iversons Snowshoe Co., 15; Kenneth C. Anderson 84; The Lakeland Times, 58, 104; Mike Knaak, 104, 105, 106; Minnesota Volunteer, 69, 72; Rev. J. P. Tanguay, 100, 101, 102; Snowtreads Inc., 6; Thomas Hollatz, 20, 26, 50, 54, 55, 56, 65, 68, 82, 85, 88; Cassie Hollatz, 23; United States Air Force, 39; Vermont Tubbs Company, 3, 4, 9, 17, 18; Corinne Ebacher, 74, 75, 76, 77, 78, 79, 80.

ISBN 0-87839-010-3

For further information address:

NORTH STAR PRESS
P.O. Box 451
St. Cloud, Minnesota 56301

The Snow Shoe Call

Here's to the slim snowshoe
In glory we renew,
Its frame will live and pleasure give
To manly hearts and true.
May its graceful dipping
The fair and brave enthral,
And with it live the echoes of
Our mountain snow shoe call.

Tull-lul-lul-li-it-too

(Chorus)
Hear the wild shout of the snow shoers!
(The call)
Ringing o'er mountain and valley!
(The call)
Dying away in the valley.

Here's to the rousing song
We sing as we tramp along,
Over the hill it bounds and trills
In echoes clear and strong,
If the strength and glory
Of youth you would recall,
Then exercise your lungs and limbs
On snow shoes with our call.

(Chorus)
Hear the wild shout of the snow shoers!

by W. G. Beers, 1874
Dedicated to the
Montreal S. S. Club

INTRODUCTION

The temperature stood at minus twenty degrees, at Minocqua, Wisconsin, as my wife, Cassie, and I trudged across the snow-crusted surface of tiny Torpy Lake. Slush was evident beneath the snow, despite the crisp cold.

We stopped at the center of the lake. The morning was quiet and clear. The sky was bright blue, without a trace of city smog. The best part of the whole scenario was the silence. Wilderness Silence. Two people comfortably alone in nature. No words were spoken, and none were needed. Then we heard — "Errrrrrrrrrrrrrrrrrrrrrrrrrrrrrrrrrrrrrrrrrrrrrrrrrrr" — in the distance.

The sound was the unforgettable whine of a snowmobile churning through the woods. The quiet beauty we were sharing was suddenly shattered. A snowmobile, perhaps the most wretched mechanical invention of all time, was drumming the silence to death.

The number of news stories tallying the deaths and the maiming injuries of people riding snowmobiles mount each week. Property and wildlife destruction is an additionally serious matter. Cabin theft in winter has increased because of easy access to remote areas by snowmobiles. Destruction of wildlife by cruel or careless "sportsmen" using snowmobiles is also on the increase. An example of this type of "sport" is flushing a deer out of the woods onto a lake, and circling around it until the deer dies of exhaustion.

To see a seven-year-old snowmobile driver whiz past going fifty miles an hour across a frozen lake, is another thrill of a snowmobile winter!

Snowmobiles, Bah! Humbug!

I'll take my modified bearpaw snowshoes and wilderness any time. I'll do my nature-loving during winter in a quiet woods. I'll do it when I can partake of nature and not destroy it. I hope this book will lead you to the pleasure of snowshoeing into a quiet, crusted white wilderness.

As a former snowmobile fan who was converted to snowshoes, there is no more perfect sport for the fun of the grey-white winter months. Snowshoeing—for the thinking man.

Thomas L. J. Hollatz
Route 1
Mann Lake Road
Boulder Junction, Wisconsin 54512

CONTENTS

THE WHITE EARTH
SNOWSHOE GUIDE BOOK

The owl, for all his feathers, was cold.
The hare limp'd trembling through the frozen grass.

John Keats
Poems 1820

Chapter One

Which Snowshoes For You?

Unless you are the famed north woods guide Porter Dean of Boulder Junction, Wisconsin, who never wears shoes much less snowshoes, you will need snowshoes to move about in any off-road deep-snow country.

Porter, who is known far and wide as "Barefoot," tromps through spring, summer, fall, and even parts of winter in bare feet. Once a mild panic began among Boulder Junction citizens when they found bear tracks in the snow outside of the Junction Bar. The bar owner got his rifle, and went searching for this fearless bear which had wandered too close to town. The bear posse's search soon ended at Porter Dean's doorstep. The bear had only been 'Barefoot' wandering through the snow in search of a beer.

With the exception of Porter Dean, ordinary mortals need some broad, weight-spreading device on their feet to help them navigate over deep snow in winter. The snowshoe allows such navigation.

The most important thing to know when shopping for snowshoes is to understand what you are buying. You will save many headaches and a lot of your hard earned dollars if you ask questions and read some books on whatever you are buying.

A friend from Minnesota tells the story about his oldest son who purchased a pair of Alaskan snowshoes without prior knowledge about the care of snowshoes. The boy brought his cold and wet webs indoors, and couldn't figure out why they twisted in half. I wouldn't have had to hear the end of the story. I knew what had happened. Any damn fool should know enough to leave good shoes outdoors, hung high out of animal reach, lest the webs turn and twist the shoes into queer shapes as the lacing dries.

His son learned an expensive lesson. The cost of a pair of snowshoes and bindings will run from thirty to fifty dollars. There is a price spread between the cheaper mass produced plastic snowshoes, for instance, and the more expensive, hand made Canadian Cree shoes.

Basically, there are four snowshoe styles: Bearpaw, Michigan or Maine, Alaskan, and Ojibwa. Outside of those four styles, there are more than seventy-three types of modifications, depending on the individual snowshoe maker's preference.

BEARPAW: *Patte d'Ours*

The standard bearpaw is called the snowshoe for all occasions. It is the best snowshoe style for those who like to wander off of the main trail, for a walk into the woods. This shoe is most noted for its ease of turning, whereas the long narrow Alaskan model can be a real handicap in the woods. There are a few flaws in the bearpaw design, but manufacturers are improvising and improving, constantly seeking perfection.

One improvement is the Westover modified bearpaw. This snowshoe looks the same as the standard bearpaw, with the exception of the rear of the shoes. A short tail has been added, and the rounded back eliminated. The modified bearpaws have found favor with the Alaskan bush pilots and snowmobilers to have as emergency equipment when their engines give out while in wilderness situations. These shoes are lightweight, and easy to transport, especially on a snowmobile.

Another improvement in the bearpaw design is the Otter or Green Mountain modified bearpaw. It keeps the rounded tail of the bearpaw shoe but it is of a narrower design and has a slight

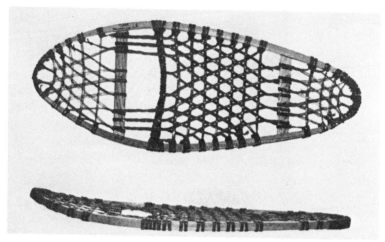

The Bearpaw

upturn at the front of the shoe. This snowshoe design is my favorite. For maneuverability, the Green Mountain can't be beaten. It is also best for rough hilly travel, where the Westover design is best for more moderate snowshoeing.

Think about where you are going to do most of your snowshoeing. Does the terrain of your chosen countryside demand the specialized design of the kind of snowshoe you plan to purchase? If you plan to use snowshoes for hilly woods terrain most of the time, then buy one of the bearpaw designs to fit your requirements.

A list of some of the bearpaw snowshoe dealers is in the appendix. Incidentally, if you ever hear an old timer refer to a set of snowshoes as "cabin models," he is probably talking about the bearpaw design.

MICHIGAN OR MAINE: *Bouts Releves*

This snowshoe design is excellent for trails and open areas. They are perhaps best suited for the open forest trails and plains.

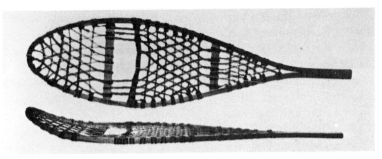

The Michigan

The two types of snowshoe are very similar to each other, and the novice snowshoer will have a hard time telling the two designs apart. Both snowshoe designs look like long tennis rackets. The point that distinguishes them, one from the other, is that the Michigan model has a rounded nose with less upturn in front, than does the Maine model, while the Maine is more pointed in front, and has more upturn. It's good for you to know which model is which, because, believe it or not, I've found dealers who couldn't tell one design from the other.

Nine out of ten times, the Maine or Michigan models are the ones you have seen on television, or hanging over a fireplace in some north woods lodge. Maine or Michigan snowshoes are excellent for long, extended use on open areas, or cleared trails.

ALASKAN: *Trappeurs*

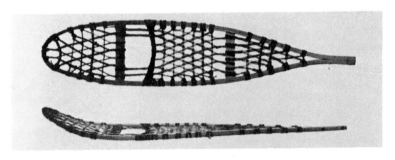

This snowshoe is also known as the pickerel, trail, or Yukon shoe. The Alaskan snowshoe is a tough, rugged shoe that is the king of travel over deep snow, and in open country. I'm sure Sergeant Preston of the Yukon used a pair of Alaskans. With his famed lead dog, Yukon King, and his trusty snowshoes, there wasn't a desperado in the Yukon who could enjoy a restful night.

The Alaskan is perhaps the most stable of all snowshoes. It is difficult to tip in these snowshoes which is one of the drawbacks of the bearpaw design. The front edge of the Alaskans are sharply upturned, which eliminates the tip from plowing down into and catching the snow.

If you ever enter a snowshoe race (which will be described in the games chapter) wearing bearpaws, and the fellow next to you has on Alaskans, and the race terrain is a flat, long open country, say "Thanks but no thanks." The Alaskan snowshoes serve as cross country skiis (a sport which is also staging a popular rebirth in the States and Canada) in open terrain.

One thing you must keep in mind about your snowshoes after use on the trail: *Ne Pas Secher trop pres du fue;* or, not too near the fire or your forty dollar pair of Alaskan snowshoes will self destruct.

OJIBWA: *Ojibway*

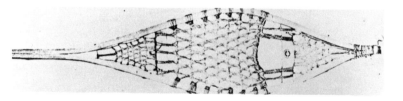

The Ojibwa snowshoe is funny looking! The shoe is tapered at the front and at the back. It looks like a double handled tennis racket. In some ways, the Ojibwa looks like the Alaskan, with no upturn at the front.

Pat Wilsie, the owner of Aqualand in Boulder Junction, Wisconsin, pointed out one great advantage the Ojibwa snowshoe has; the pointed style knifes through deep snow, which makes for easier forward mobility on the trail. Wilsie also reminded me that the Ojibwa design does not pile up with snow, which can literally be a real drag.

Famed artist Frederic Remington, in his drawings of the old west, depicted snowshoes in which both tail and toe were brought together to form a point, doing away with the difficult task of bending wood to form a curved toe. The frame was strengthened by two or three crossbars. Remington was painting the Ojibwa style snowshoe.

The above snowshoes are the basic styles. The newer styles will be explained now.

PLASTIC:

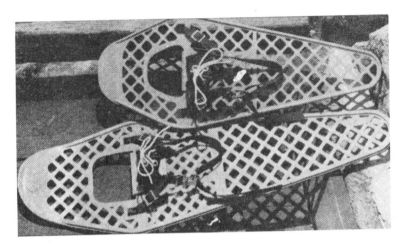

The plastic snowshoe is gaining in popularity. It is especially liked by snowmobilers for added safety protection in case their arctic attackers explode while deep in some woods. Most of the plastic snowshoes I have seen are designed after the basic bear-paw, which makes for compact carrying. The most popular ones are the Snowtreads, which are distributed by Sportsmen Products. The shoes complete with bindings sell for $25.90 a pair. The Snowtreads people have experimented with bindings on the present model for six years, and have developed an adjustable nylon binding which will fit all boot sizes. The binding prevents lateral heel movement, which is a common problem of other bindings. The lack of heel side-motion helps to cut down fatigue during wood hikes. Their new binding is designed to fit all models of snowshoes, and not just for the Snowtreads, which may prove to be a separate bonanza on the Snowtreads sales charts.

The Snowtreads are made from a lightweight cold weather plastic, developed by the Eastman Chemical Company. The plastic construction greatly reduces the price of the snowshoe, a big plus for the buyer.

According to one snowshoe authority, one negative factor is that the plastic snowshoes have the tendency to tilt back in the snow, kicking snow up the back of the leg.

After testing these snowshoes for three hours, I found little or no tilt, but I did find that the snow was kicked up against the back of my legs. Another plus for the owner is the low cost of maintenance. I recommend Snowtreads, especially to have along for an emergency situation. The Tubbs firm also distributes a plastic set of snowshoes.

ALUMINUM:

The aluminum frame snowshoes offer one great advantage over any wooden snowshoes in that they are extremely light. They are made of extruded aluminum framing with rawhide lacing. One of the manufacturers of this model, Black Forest Enterprises,

Snowshoer using aluminum frame snowshoes.

recommends them for trailpack hikes or mountaineering. They are a durable, hardy snowshoe. The Black Forest firm sells them in kits, which can be a money saver. The kits can be assembled in four to five hours. No special tools are required to complete the kit. The entire snowshoe is coated with polyester resin, to protect the lacing against abrasion. Additional protective coats of resin can be added as needed.

The bindings are of Neoprene-nylon, a tough nylon fabric bonded between two layers of Neoprene rubber. This binding is strong, and will not absorb water. A binding of this nature will not freeze up, ice over, or stretch. The one size outfit will adjust to fit anyone from 80 to 250 pounds.

MAGNESIUM:

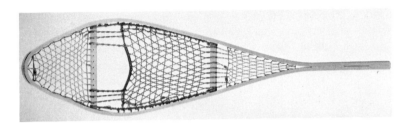

These snowshoes have been developed by the United States and Canadian military forces. They are extremely light, and have a webbing of nylon covered aircraft control cable. The cost factor is very high, and is the main reason they are eliminated from civilian sporting consideration.

Shoes of magnesium (raquettes de magnesium) are available from the Magline firm of Renfrew, Ontario, Canada. The frame offers welded construction, and is made of high strength aircraft grade magnesium alloy extrusion, hot formed to shape.

The magnesium snowshoe is 48 inches long, and 12.25 inches wide. The standard model weighs 2.25 pounds. There is no stretch or sag with the magnesium snowshoe. They also are rodent and rust proof, and rated at seven times the service life of wooden snowshoes. They also will not pick up moisture. It is a super snowshoe, but too damn costly.

WALLINGFORD:

This is a relatively new design in snowshoes. The Wallingford, which is named after the town of Wallingford, Vermont, the home of Tubbs Snowshoes, combines the best of the Green Mountain bearpaw and the Michigan. Its shape, and short tail make it versatile, adapting well to both woods and trail. The

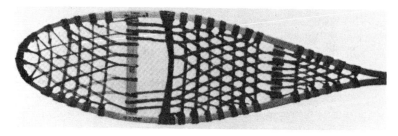

The Wallingford

split tail prevents brush from snagging the shoe. The Wallingford is suited for any person up to two hundred pounds. The Green Mountain bearpaw just referred to is also manufactured by Vermont Tubbs, Incorporated. The Tubbs people claim the Green Mountain bearpaw is the most versatile snowshoe on the market.

ALGONQUIN:

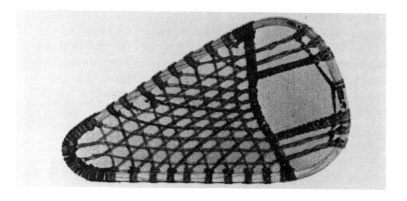

This snowshoe was originally developed for loggers in the northeast. The Algonquin also has become popular with the snowmobilers. It is well balanced, and because of the placement of the toe cord, will not dig into snow. The Algonquin snowshoe fits easily onto most snowmobiles. The snowshoe is small in size, and it will support persons up to 225 pounds.

The snowshoes listed are basic ones, and may or may not include some snowshoe model you have seen. There is probably some old timer hibernating in the north woods with a special design made from old whiskey kegs, or a few other hybrid designs which I have failed to hear about.

It would be impossible to describe every variation of the bearpaw, Michigan, Alaskan, or Ojibwa snowshoe. Every manufacturer turns up a new wrinkle which distinguishes his product from the next snowshoe manufacturer. In any case, they are all working to improve their snowshoes which in the end can only benefit the outdoorsman. It would be impossible to recommend one brand or style of snowshoe over another just as it would be impossible to tell someone to drive a Cadillac when he prefers an Imperial. If you want bearpaw snowshoes for the open trail, buy them. There is no law that says you can't buy a bearpaw snowshoe although the snow terrain might dictate a Michigan model. Buy what you want and from whom you want. Buy something you will use and your shoes won't be a waste of money.

The number of different kinds of snowshoes would probably range in the hundreds. Even the basic snowshoe webbing is changing each year as some manufacturer comes out with a new material like Neoprene—which is the webbing material I have on my modified bearpaws.

Indians used caribou and moose hides for webbing on their snowshoes. Caribou and moose is reported to be the best material for snowshoe webbing, according to one source. Caribou and moose has been replaced by rawhide (cattle), nylon cord, Neoprene, plastic, and other webbing modifications.

Rawhide is a favorite snack of mice which is a great disadvantage, especially if you store your snowshoes in your cabin in the woods. After the mice have feasted on your snowshoe rawhide, the cost to have snowshoes restrung will be almost as high as the cost of your original purchase.

Nylon makes an excellent webbing. However, the nylon webbing will fray badly if the snowshoer travels over a snowfield filled with exposed rocks or other abrasive obstacles.

Neoprene resists mouse attack. Underground wiring experts also have discovered the rodent-resistant quality of Neoprene. They are using more and more Neoprene instead of costly steel cable for their underground connections. Neoprene snowshoe webbing resists snow buildup during the wet snow condition, and will have a longer life than rawhide. There are some snowshoe purists who will demand nothing but rawhide for it's own sake. Neoprene is very strong and will not absorb water. It will not freeze, ice up, or stretch.

THE WHITE EARTH

The sport of snowshoeing is making an impressive comeback in the United States and Canada. With new ecological concern in our everyday lives, the use of snowshoes becomes a matter of serious consideration for winter outdoorsmen.

Many communities have, because of economic reasons, opened trails for snowmobilers, but the snowshoers will have to do a little demanding to gain trails for themselves. If you're hiking on a snowmobile trail while wearing snowshoes, and hear that "Errrrrrrrrrrrrrrrrrrr," it can only mean one thing—get out of the way quickly! Someone on a snowmobile has to get to the next tavern quickly. Hell hath no fury like a snowmobile pack headed for the next beer.

One experience my wife and I had comes to mind. Last winter we were having dinner at a supper club in western Wisconsin. We were enjoying a delicious duck dinner, while a snowmobile pack, twenty in all, was toasting the fact that they had made it to the place from the last bar, without anyone being maimed or killed. After an hour, they decided to crank up. As they were readying to leave, someone dropped a quarter into the juke box. That stopped them in their tracks, and they returned to the bar for another round of quickies. As they left, an hour later, the bar owner yelled out, "Be sure to turn right." The turn would have taken them back to the lodge where they were staying.

"We know the way," one yelled back. The snowmobile rat pack leader led his herd of snowmobiles out of the driveway, and promptly gunned off to the left!

Earlier, on that same day, a snowmobile rider in St. Paul, Minnesota, crashed his machine into the side of a freight train, fatally mincing himself and his machine.

I am not leading a hell fire crusade against the snowmobile; they do have their advantages, especially in emergency situations. Winter used to be such a long, dull affair in the cold northland. The snowmobile has opened the north country up to new economic and recreational pursuits. I only hope the track wounds can be healed.

Last winter, I talked with a tavern owner who rented snowmobiles at Woodruff, Wisconsin, concerning the blight of the snowmobile in the northland. The tavern owner took an insouciant quaff of his brew, and looked at me. "Don't apologize," he said. "I agree that the snowmobile is a menace to humans and wildlife. If I had my way, I'd outlaw the damn things. However, it's the only way I can keep my doors open in winter."

[Pardon my disgression, but my bias against snowmobiles makes my pen want to say some terrible things.]

Ben Thoma, writing in the November-December 1970 issue of *Conservation Volunteer*, lists common North American snowshoes of the eighteenth and nineteenth centuries.

He lists six categories:

Salish or Bearpaw

Single piece of willow in oval or round shape, held together with rawhide square webbing pattern.

Abnaki or Huron-Iroquois

One piece frame, pointed at heel and braced with one or two crossbars, webbing hexagonal.

Naskapı

Two piece frame, spliced at rounded toe, with medium tail and hexagonal webbing.

Athapaskan, pointed toe

Two piece frame, lashed identically at toe and tail.

Athapaskan, round toe

Two piece frame with toe spliced and hide wrapped to form round toe.

Wooden Snowshoes

Various kinds, the most common in Canada being round or oval plank, often used for travel on melting snow.

THE SNOWSHOER'S CODE

1. Keep off closed trails, and out of posted areas.
2. Always lend a helping hand when you see someone in distress.
3. Do not leave your litter on trails or in camping areas.
4. Make yourself available to search and rescue parties.
5. Do not damage living trees, shrubs, or other natural features.
6. Do not pollute streams or lakes.
7. Know and respect your own limitations while using snowshoes.
8. Understand and respect all wildlife.
9. Keep your gar in good condition.
10. Have fun.

I please myself with the graces
of winter scenery, and believe
that we are as much touched by it
as by the genial influences of summer.

Ralph Waldo Emerson, *Nature*

Chapter Two

Snowshoe Bindings

The first time I tried to put my feet into snowshoe bindings was a semi-disaster. My novice attempt was a mess. It was a mess because I didn't know what I was doing. I hope after reading this chapter, you will suffer the same problems I did—it will be good for you!

Perhaps the simplest of all snowshoe bindings is the combination of a leather heel strap and wide toe piece with a cross strap over the instep. This binding could be self-made, but I only recommend it for the real pro who is extremely handy with tools.

Avoid headaches—purchase a good set of commercial bindings. The commercial snowshoe bindings will have a buckle fitted to the heel strap. It is important that you adjust this buckle on the outside of your foot, below the ankle bone.

Make sure your commercial binding is equipped with straps long enough so that they can be crossed behind the heel and securely tied across the instep. Tie or buckle the strap about where you would normally tie your street shoes. When it's colder than the hinges of hell, you may find the tying of leather a little difficult. Take your time and do it right the first time. The problem of cold-weather tying has been somewhat eliminated with the development of neoprene bindings. Since neoprene bindings will not absorb water, they cannot freeze and stiffen, which makes securing a binding in cold weather a simple task.

The seller should show you the proper method of getting into your bindings when you purchase your snowshoes. If he doesn't show you, or doesn't know how, something is wrong. It would be best to shop elsewhere for your snowshoe gear.

Earlier, I mentioned the nylon binding developed by the Snowtreads people which I have found to be most suitable. This binding also helps reduce heel sway, stabilizing the snowshoe by keeping your foot centered on the webs.

Another interesting binding arrangement is one made by Iverson's Snowshoe Company. Their nylon binding is made of reinforced neoprene; it is waterproof, non-freezing, and offers positive foot control. The Iverson binding, because of the neoprene material, is a little easier to tie in a cold snap. The harness is equipped with a slide fastener and standard buckles. It is a working binding that is adjustable to any boot or shoe.

I let a friend, who had never seen a snowshoe, much less try one on, try my Iverson binding to see if he could figure it out. No problem at all! He figured it out, stepped right into the binding, tightened the instep buckle first and then adjusted the ankle buckle and was ready to go.

The Iverson snowshoes are made with a webbing of nylon-reinforced neoprene stitched to the shoe frames of Northern white ash. This firm claims their webbing outwears the conventional rawhide lace bindings, two to one. This hasn't been proven yet as the nylon-neoprene combination hasn't been around that long. The thing I like about the Iverson's bindings is that the lacing does not soak up moisture, become wet and sag. Nor will this binding coat with ice and snow. No application of waterproofing

THE WHITE EARTH

material is necessary to maintain the original appearance, strength, and tautness of the Iverson binding. The snowshoer's most common problem is that of wet, soggy snowshoe lacing. I have found Iverson's to be one of the best of all the snowshoe binding manufacturers. This is not a plug but rather my objective evaluation of a fine product. There are no better snowshoe bindings made.

Iverson's Neoprene bindings.

I mentioned the matter of heel control. The Bastien Brothers firm offers a heel control binding called *Heel-Kon-Trol*. Their heel control harness is an aluminum and stainless steel footplate fitted with leather straps. There are foot pivot points at the forward binding tips and crossbars where these bindings are screwed to the snowshoe frames (if the snowshoe model is rather slim). The pivot attachment is made directly to the lacing of the wider models such as bearpaws. A leather toe strap is attached to the cord separately from the rest of the binding.

If tied too tightly, as I have found, toe bindings can be rough on your foot, cramping the foot like some Chinese torture device. Bastien bindings, unlike the others, can be tied rather loosely.

As can be seen in the illustration, another locking strap passes under the heel at the back of the harness. It attaches to the buckle on the outside. That strap keeps the heel secure at the attaching point. This heel strap practically eliminates tiresome slipping around in the bindings, keeping the snowshoes in line with the feet which, after you have become more efficient on snowshoes, you will find is a real help on the long trail. Although the Bastien bindings keep the snowshoes in line with the feet, they have one minor disadvantage—they are heavy. When you gain the advantage of keeping your snowshoes in line, you lose with an increase in weight. Take your pick—light bindings and heel slippage or heavy bindings and little or no slippage.

Heel-Kon-Trol binding designed by the Bastien Brothers Inc., Village Huron, Quebec, Canada.

Uncle Sam's army equipment research people have developed a rather conventional binding and for a time these could be purchased very reasonably at surplus stores. When snowshoe buffs got wind that these bindings were available, most were snapped up quickly. There still might be a few around—it is worth having a look. Leather and metal components make up the army binding. A leather toe piece is attached to the foot rest which is a metal plate. A hinge passes through the plate at its fore-edge just above the toe cord. Metal straps are used to secure the pin. The metal

THE WHITE EARTH

straps are bent around the frontal crossbar. The army has also experimented with crust spikes located along the toe hole to aid in forward thrust.

The Tubbs Company offers four types of bindings, all of which are rated as excellent.

Their Type "H" which costs $6.50, is a good general-use binding and is popular with recreational snowshoer. The full instep provides extra support. The Tubbs' Howe model binding costs $10.00 and is a heavy-control binding recommended for

Tubbs Type H — Good binding for general use and is popular with recreational snowshoers.

Tubbs Howe Style Binding — Heavy control type of binding for those on snowshoes for a long period of time.

those who will be on snowshoes for long periods of time. The Howe features a toe cup which prevents forward movement of the foot. The Tubbs Neoprene costs $8.75 and is gaining in popularity. Some woodsmen consider it the best binding on the market since it is light and gives excellent support against both forward and lateral motion. The Type "A" costs $5.50; it is simple and well-liked by recreational snowshoers. It has a tapered toe piece which provides good protection against forward foot movement.

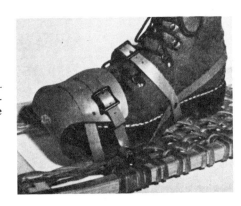

Tubbs Neoprene Binding — Considered by many professional woodsmen to be the best binding on the market.

Tubbs Type A — One of the better tie bindings on the market. It is a good binding for loose snow conditions.

If you are the kind of character who cries everytime you spend a dollar and you refuse to purchase a man-made commercial binding, you can always improvise a simple binding.

A short rope attached from the toe portion of your boot to the master cord plus a heel holding device cut from an old inner tube is perhaps the cheapest binding. Surprisingly, it works!

For additional facts and tips on snowshoe bindings I can recommend an excellent book entitled *The Snowshoe Book* by William Osgood and Leslie Hurley. It is available from the Stephen Greene Press, Brattleboro, Vermont. *The Last Whole Earth Catalog* and *The Snowshoe Book* are really the only good sources, with the exception of this book, to learn about the beautiful sport of snowshoeing.

After adjusting your bindings and breaking them in, perhaps you will want to experiment. Many snowshoers remove the heel strap and replace them with an inner tube rubber band as mentioned earlier for a simple binding.

Herman Smith, University of Wisconsin extension agent for area recreation resources at Rhinelander, Wisconsin, reports there are many woodsmen who wouldn't use anything else for a heel strap but a piece of old inner tube.

When Smith was a rookie snowshoer, Ranger Zagorski, a forester, told him to use a wide strip of inner tube to place around his ankle for support. Smith vows, "It steadied my ankles and avoided broken legs during my many novice falls."

"I often asked what made the shoe webbing stretch," Smith said. "There are several reasons. One is that when the webbing becomes wet on socalled 'warm' days (above zero), the leather thongs will give and it is most important not to dry them by a fire as they will become very brittle."

"Leave the shoes standing upright to air dry even though they may freeze. There must be stretch in snowshoe bindings and lacing to allow for uneven surfaces when you walk on or traverse over brush, branches, or other natural obstacles."

"We always oiled our webbing with neatsfoot oil at the start of the season, again during mid-winter and again at the end of the season. We used clear spar varnish on the wood frames, being careful not to get too much on the leather," Smith added.

Never leave your snowshoes stacked in the snow outside of the cabin at night as small animals will feast on the rawhide.

The lacing and harness should be occasionally de-iced. Hang your shoes high on the outside wall of the cabin until dry and then hang the shoes up under the porch roof of your cabin to remain cool to outside temperature, ready to crack another snow trail.

Early trappers used a harness or binding called a "Montagnais hitch" (named after the Montagnard Indians, a tribe of Athapaskan Indians which inhabited the Canadian Rockies).

The Montagnais hitch was made from common one-inch wide oil lamp wicking and would usually last an entire trapping season, according to Ben Thoma in the November-December, 1970, issue of *Conservation Volunteer*.

Snowshoe bindings are a matter of personal choice. They are as varied as the many snowshoe designs. The simple "lamp-wicking hitch" is good although the beginner may have difficulty fitting it for the first time.

A snowshoer wll certainly want two things in his bindings:
1. Enough rigidity to be able to make a turn on the snow-shoe easily.
2. A design that won't let the snow pack and build up under the foot.

A properly fastened binding. Note position of boot.

"I love snow, and all the forms
Of the radiant frost."

Song to the Men of England
Percy Bysshe Shelley

Chapter Three

What To Wear

It was imperative a couple of years ago that skiers had to dress the role of a millionaire off on a jet-set Swiss holiday. The most exotic winter fashions were the in thing. Perhaps it was sequins on ski clothes that turned the outdoor fashion world on its ear. The cost factor, especially for skiers, is marginally exorbitant.

Jerry Shanley, manager of the Playboy Ski Hill at Lake Geneva, Wisconsin, commented in the *Chicago Tribune:* "You know why skiing caught on? Clothes. We often get girls in this bar who never ski, but they have nice clothes. And if you put a dime in their pocket, believe me, you know if its heads or tails."

By the time a skier clothes himself from head to toe, a three-hundred dollar tab is a minimum of cost and this before hitting the slopes. At some time during the last two years someone said,

"Enough already!" to fancy clothes for the outdoors. The change to practical, cheap clothing for winter sports is creating another boon with not-so-cheap blue jeans, strange as it may seem, being the hottest selling item of all.

Skiers now consider it "super" to wear jeans on the slopes—temperatures permitting. When it gets too cold, a good pair of sweat pants are just the thing. I purchased my pair on sale at Montgomery Wards for $2.98. Here's a practical hint—spray your jeans and sweat pants with Scotchgard fabric protector. There is nothing more miserable than to be wet and cold during a winter fun day.

Cross-country skiers wear knickers to allow for free leg movement. Some cross-country fans are switching to the jeans as they can be tied up to resemble an "el cheapo" pair of knickers.

As for snowshoers, wear comfortable but warm clothing. Tight fitting trousers are more of a hindrance than a help. Winter clothing should b light and loose. You may find that if you are overdressed you will sweat. Good old itchy wool is still one of the best shirt materials in the cold, especially when you know that you will really exert yourself. A good trick with a wool shirt is to face the inside of the collar with a silk or rayon band. This will reduce the neck irritation from the rough wool.

A cross-country ski buff friend swears by a fish-net under-shirt—you know, the kind you have seen in those outdoor sports catalogs and wondered what kind of guy would wear that thing! Over the fish-net shirt he wears a light windbreaker. The theory, he claims is to allow evaporation of perspiration before it can soak into the clothing.

My cross-country buddy, in wearing only the windbreaker, feels that when he gets cold, he can always get warmer by exerting himself.

I wear a T-shirt, wool shirt, a sweater (which, when you're too hot, can be removed during a rest break) and a well-insulated light jacket. This combination feels light and it is comfortable. Over my bottom half I wear a pair of long woolies and trousers of smooth wool, so snow will not stick to them. Proper dress for snowshoeing consists of the "layer system" topped off with an artic-type shell parka.

Pat Snook, writing in *National Wildlife* magazine, tells of his method for getting set to go outdoors in winter.

The Compleat Snowshoer.

"A cotton T-shirt, followed by a medium-weight wool shirt, loose sweater and the parka. If it's very cold, I may add an old cotton dress shirt or knit polo shirt between the first two. With this combination, if you start to overheat, you can pull off the sweater and stuff it in your rucksack or tie it around your waist, and open up the other layers by unbuttoning."

Ski pants are fine to keep your lower half warm. Snook, however, perfers a slightly baggy pair of wind resistant trousers over loose flannel pajama bottoms.

Another helpful hint is to wear suspenders to shift the weight of clothing from your waist to the shoulders. If flannel pajamas aren't your bag, then buy some good thermal underwear. There are excellent brands of thermal underwear on the market. Make sure your trousers-boot link is secure and snow proof. With ski pants, the problem of wet socks is all but eliminated.

One of life's little annoyances H. L. Mencken forgot to mention, along with a woman's laugh at the wrong time, is cold, wet and soggy socks. A further item that will irk a snowshoer when outdoors in winter is a shirttail that always pops out. When you bend over to fix a loose snowshoe binding and your shirttail pops out, your back will be exposed to the cold. Many of the mail order catalogs feature wool shirts with an extra long tail. Buy one. It'll put you one tail ahead of the game. A last resort shirttail can be made by adding six inches of flannel to the bottom of the regular shirt tail. There will be plenty of long shirt tail to tuck and hold by this little trick.

Mittens:

Mittens are next. They are excellent for warmth, far better than gloves. Do not buy gloves, even ski gloves, as the fingers get extremely cold during a long trail hike. Two pairs of mittens are best—inner liner and outer shell. The mitten most preferred is the gauntlet or long cuffed.

Most mittens made for snowmobilers have the gauntlet feature. The cuffs keep the snow on the outside—where it belongs. Cuffs also provide a wind lock between jacket and hand cover, keeping the wrists dry and warm.

Footwear

Although Nancy Sinatra once sang that boots are made for walking, she should have added that boots are made for snowshoers to keep their feet warm.

A flat soled boot is generally recommended. It cuts wear and distributes your weight over as much of the webbing as possible. Shoepac boots (leather uppers and rubber bottoms) are excellent for use with snowshoes. My favorite shoepac is the Sorel Arctic boot with felt liners. Always buy an extra pair of liners because after a day on the trail a felt liner will become wet. A spare pair will allow you to keep your feet warm and dry. Wet feet blister easily and obviously chill much quicker.

When it's likely to be cold and wet, I recommend wool or orlon socks inside the waterproof or rubberized boots. When winter conditions are cold and dry, revert to light orlon or wool socks. The light socks take care of the problem of sweating feet by absorbing the perspiration. Insulated leather boots also can be used, but I don't recommend them.

Many snowshoers, especially in Canada, wear a lightweight boot with a mocassin-like leather bottom and canvas top made especially for snowshoe use.

Headwear

A visored, waterproof hat is recommended. A knit pull-over hat is handy as it can be pulled down over the ears when the temperature dips. The traditional snowshoer's headgear is the knitted *toque* (took). This colorful pull-over is made of bright yarns and topped with a tassel. It generally does not have a visor.

Sun Goggles

Never venture outdoors for a full day of snowshoeing during winter without sun goggles. It's a good but strict rule to follow. When the sun reflects off of bright white snow, you could be in danger of becoming snow blinded. Snow blindness can also happen when it is cloudy and overcast.

I use a pair of ski goggles with two interchangeable lenses —one yellow and one dark green. The green lenses are for bright sunlight, and the yellow lenses if the sky is cloudy and you want to brighten your perspective.

One symptom of snowblindness is a burning sensation in the eyes. The eyes may feel somewhat sandy. Other symptoms are described in the chapter on winter survival.

Costs

Here are some comparative costs between snowmobiling, cross country skiing, and snowshoeing.

Snowmobiling		Cross Country Skiing		Snowshoeing	
machine	$800.00 and up	skiis	$80.00	snowshoes & bindings	$35.00
suit	45.00	poles	15.00	knit hat	2.00
helmet	15.00	boots	35.00	goggles	3.00
mittens	5.00	pants	25.00	boots	30.00
boots	20.00	jacket	35.00	jacket	35.00
insurance	50.00	knit hat	2.00	trousers	
gas, oil	200.00	goggles	3.00	(wool)	20.00
(season) to	400.00	mittens	12.00	suspenders	4.00
socks	2.95	misc.	20.00	socks	2.95
underwear	6.00	TOTAL	$227.00	mittens	5.00
goggles	3.00			TOTAL	$136.95
TOTAL	$1,446.95				

Cold weather wardrobe — Parka, wool pants, and boots that cover the legs of the pants to keep the snow out.

> The most beautiful thing we can
> experience is the mysterious. It
> is the source of all true art and science.
>
> Albert Einstein
> *What I Believe,* in Forum Oct., 1930

Chapter Four

Snowshoe Mechanics

Snowshoes, or *raquettes* as the Canadians call them, and how they work are best described by Edward Rossit in *Snow Camping and Mountaineering.*

"If we say that the area of the bottom of the boot is about 50 square inches . . . and if we say that a man weighs 200 pounds, then by simple arithmetic we can calculate that such a man with such a small boot will exert a pressure of four pounds per square inch on the snow. This is more pressure than soft snow will resist, and down goes our 200-pound traveler."

"Obviously, if this same man could exert less pressure on the snow, he might not sink so deep. Obviously also, he cannot reduce his weight by a half or even a quarter. But if he can increase the area on the snow over which he exerts this pressure, this will reduce the pressure per square inch. This is the principle upon which the snowshoes work . . . "

"Going again to good round numbers, a bearpaw snowshoe has an area of about 300 square inches. A trail model snowshoe has an area of about 600 square inches. If we take our same 200-pound man and put him on bearpaws, he will now exert a pressure of .67 pounds per square inch. On trail model snowshoes (Alaskans or Michigans) he will exert a pressure of .33 pounds per square inch, or about five ounces. These pressures are considerably less than the four pounds per square inch which he exerts on the surface of his snow with only his boots. Usually, this difference is enough to prevent a man from sinking into the snow, and allows him to walk on the surface without floundering."

A snowshoe of about thirteen inches across at the widest part and of about forty-eight inches long will easily support a 170-pound adult. In keeping with the feminine lib movement, snowshoe designs are the same for the women. As many won't readily admit to a weight of 170 pounds, the gals can usually pick up somewhat smaller snowshoes.

Figure roughly 12 x 46 inches of snowshoe for 150 pounds of avid winter sportsman and 11 x 40 of shoe for 100 pounds of the avid same. The real figure comes to about four square inches of snowshoe per pound of avid same, so be honest when sizing up a new set of snowshoes. Remember, the weight of your outer garments will count towards the total snowshoe load.

Check for center of balance when you purchase a set of snowshoes. Make sure that there is enough weight behind the pivot point of your snowshoe bindings. The snowshoe's tail may lift when you pick up your foot, allowing the toe part to dig in. When the toe of your snowshoe digs in, or plows, you will probably wind up in the snow on your nose. That's why snowshoe balance is so important. Ease of use and safety is the goal. Besides, it really is difficult to get up on your feet again after a headlong tumble into a drift of deep powdery snow.

The use of ski poles or balance poles might be warrented in some snow conditions. The poles can help you from floundering in deep snow, or provide balance when traversing hills. These poles can be purchased at any snow sport shop. The cost is minimal and well worth the expense in certain conditions.

SNOWSHOE SIZE GUIDE

weight (in pounds)	size (in inches)
Bearpaw - modified (the "Westover" style)	
125 — 150	12 x 34
150 — 180	13 x 35
180 — 210	14 x 35
Bearpaw - modified (the "Green Mountain" style)	
up to 200	10 x 36
Bearpaw - standard	
150 — 175	14 x 30
175 — 200	15 x 30
175 — 200	13 x 33
200 — 250	14 x 36
Maine	
35 — 50	9 x 30
50 — 60	10 x 36
60 — 90	11 x 40
100 — 125	12 x 42
125 — 150	12 x 48
150 — 175	13 x 48
175 — 200	14 x 48
Michigan	
150 — 175	13 x 48
175 — 200	14 x 48
200 — 250	14 x 52
Alaskan	
125 — 150	10 x 48
150 — 175	10 x 56
175 — 200	12 x 60

Snowshoer using poles to help maintain balance. Poles are very helpful in heavy snow conditions.

This man has the correct snow-shoe for his size and weight.

"We'll use a signal I have tried and found far-reaching and easy to yell. Waa-hoo"

The Last of the Plainsmen
Zane Grey

Chapter Five

Wilderness Trouble

Snowshoeing is one of the easiest and safest sports ever invented. Yet there are unexpected dangers for anybody in the wilderness. Anyone can get lost in the grey-white snow country, even an experienced outdoorsman and it is best that you prepare for emergencies that might befall you.

If you become lost in the woods during the winter you must be prepared to survive. Winter is extremely harsh on those people foolish enough to venture into the wilderness unprepared and unable to accept conditions as winter dictates. Before you go out snowshoeing, skiing, or snowmobiling, you should inform someone where you will be going and how long you will be gone. Stay out only as long as you indicated because if you become lost or injured it is very important that rescue operations begin as soon as possible. The person you tell where you are going should be informed that if you are not back in a prescribed time, he should begin rescue operations.

If you should become lost or injured in the woods your life can depend on the fact that you can control your fear and panic. The first word in winter survival is psychology. Think about your predicament carefully, weighing each decision. Your life depends on your mind. Whatever your situation is do something to keep yourself occupied. If you remain inactive fear will get the better of you.

Once you have fear and panic under control you must contend with your environment. Although keeping control of your mental processes is essential, your survival also depends on how you cope with your environment. The winter environment is harsh and unacceptable to unprotected human life.

The major problem in winter survival is to remain dry and protected from the cold. Insulation is the key to survival in winter. Animals who inhabit freezing climates use their insulating winter pelts to keep their body temperatures above the point of water. Human beings are very susceptible to the cold. The reason is that you and I are more than seventy percent water. If the water in our body freezes, ice crystals form which can puncture and kill the living cells. This is what happens in cases of frostbite.

When you go snowshoeing, dress as if you are going to stay in the woods for several days. This preventative measure will insure that you will have some protection from exposure if you get lost or hurt while you are in the woods. If it is a warm day and you are in the woods, take along an extra parka and some heavy gloves. You can carry these in your knapsack. Winter often changes weather conditions in a matter of hours and if you are wearing light clothing, you could be in serious trouble.

Your clothing alone is sufficient to keep your body warm if the air is still and you are not lost. If you are lost, the best way to keep out the cold is to build a shelter. Building a shelter when you are lost has a two-fold benefit. It will help you retain body heat, and it prevents you from wandering around aimlessly, becoming even more disoriented.

A lean-to shelter is fairly easy to build. Such a wind break shelter is adequate to sustain yourself for a few days, or until the wind direction changes. Lean-tos are designed for wind protection, and they are not shelters against the snow. Begin making a lean-to by finding two trees fairly close together, with low-lying branches that are easy to reach. Set a horizontal pole between two trees, resting on the supporting branches in the trees at a height of four to five feet from the ground. Straight limbs are then leaned from the ground against the horizontal pole at a forty-five degree angle to the ground. Spaces between the limbs can be filled with branches, dead leaves, twigs, or any other available material.

It is also possible to make a lean-to A-frame shelter. Repeat the single-sided lean-to construction on the other side, and you have an A-frame which resembles a pup tent. You can also make

A-frame shelter construction using cut branches and lashed together.

a lean-to against a large fallen log. The space will be snug and tight when the principle of the lean-to is applied.

A snow cave is another form of good wind protection, and it may be dug anywhere, provided there is deep snow. Although temporary, it does offer excellent protection. Don't worry about being cold, the Eskimos have used the snow igloo for centuries, and it hasn't hurt them.

Select a high snow drift, and on the side away from the wind, dig into the bottom of the drift. Dig horizontally until you have a entrance hole about three feet in diameter; dig upwards at forty-five degrees, and then carve out a sleeping platform. You can carve out a comfortable wind-proof area. Remember, if you make a snow cave, to pop an air vent through the roof for fresh air. In the cave, you can even sleep on your snowshoes to give you insulation space if needed. All the comforts of home!

A snow cave in use. Note small openning.

When using a lean-to or a snow cave, you must remember that rescue people will have a hard time spotting your shelter. You must do something to make yourself as visible as possible. It is important to remember the cardinal rule for being lost in the woods. DON'T MOVE AROUND. Stay put, and let the rescue party find you. You increase your chances of exposure and death if you actively try to find your way out of an unfamiliar woods. There are things that you can do to help rescue parties find you in the woods.

Aircraft, for the most part, are used today to help track down a sportsman or survivor lost in the woods. The number two rule to follow when you are lost in deep woods is to make yourself clearly visible from the air. The best thing to do is to find an open area and tramp out the letters SOS or HELP. Make the letters big, thirty feet in height at the minimum. Try to leave ten yards between each letter. After tramping your signal, fill in the areas stamped out with evergreen limbs, rocks, or anything that will make your signal more visible from the air. Be careful not to track the area too much in this process. Included in this chapter are additional ground-to-air signals which are copied from the United States Army Field Manual on Survival, on F. A. A. Aviation charts.

Brightly colored or conspicuous clothing is a good way to get noticed. Lay a brightly colored piece of cloth on the ground to attract attention. Fire is always a good way to attract a search party for fire can be seen for long distances. Damp leaves or green branches can be put on the fire to make it give off a heavy smoke which is a good daylight signal.

At night try signalling with a flashlight. A little beam of light pierces a long way through a dark woods. Flash three dots —or short blinks, then three dashes—or longer blinks, and then three more dots. This is the emergency signal in the international Morse code. Even if a person seeing the blinking light doesn't know Morse code, his curiosity should bring him to you, solving the "being lost" problem. Again, don't panic and begin running about in circles, using up energy. *Sit tight by your fire, and let help find you.* In daytime, during a clear sunny day, a mirror, or some polished surface will act as a good sunlight reflector. If you don't have a mirror, a tin can will also reflect a signal from the sun to a search plane. Use a knife or some other sharp instrument to punch a small hole in the middle of the tin, and use that small hole as a sighting device. Don't count on the reflector signal for the angle of reflection must be just right for a pilot to note the signal.

If you are going to have to stay in the woods for any considerable length of time, you are going to need a fire. There are so many varied ways of starting a fire, that the best advice to give you here is to remember to bring matches from home. Matches are an essential part of any survival kit. To protect matches from getting wet, simply dip the heads of stick matches in melted paraffin wax. Let them cool and place the matches in an ordinary pill container. These containers can be obtained at any local drug store. Tape a small piece of sand paper to the side of the pill bottle to make a dry striker for the waxed matches.

Tinder is not essential to a survival kit, but it comes in handy at times when the woods are wet, and dry sticks or tinder cannot be found. Find a small box or metal container that is or can be made watertight. Fill it full of wood shavings or other things that will light easily. Throw in a flint, and a piece of steel or an old file as an added precaution against using all of your matches. It is best to practice the flint and steel fire starting method at home. Trying flint and steel for the first time while lost in the cold woods is a losing proposition.

An excellent fire starter can be made from old paper pulp egg cartons, wax and wood shavings. Fill an egg carton with the wood shavings, and pour melted wax over the shavings. When the wax cools, break the individual eggholders apart. This fire starter works extremely well with wet wood or damp ground. Carry a few of these fire starters in your survival kit, and you should have no trouble starting a fire.

It is obvious to say that being prepared for survival by proper packing can make the difference between life and death. When travelling in the woods on snowshoes, it is always best to carry a map and compass, flashlight, first aid kit, waterproof matches, and emergency rations.

A survival kit is light in weight and inexpensive to make. The kit should include strong but pliable soft iron or brass wire; fishline, about fifty feet; hooks and sinkers; a sharp knife; cloth or electrical tape, a space blanket [cost: $12.00]; emergency rations; a small wire saw; and a compass and detail map of the area you are travelling through.

Survival kits can be purchased in most outfitting stores. The Gokey Company of St. Paul, Minnesota, offers a trail survival kit for $3.89, which is an adequate kit. It's compact and will fit nicely into your pocket. The kit contains matches, all-weather fire starters, a compass, three fortified chocolate bars, a fishing kit, snare wire, cooking foil, insect repellent, soap tissues, a signal whistle, a razor blade, first aid kit, ground to air signal code, and complete survival instructions. All of these items are contained in a heavy duty, weather-tight, re-sealable vinyl pouch. It weighs six ounces.

The best single food ration to have with you on the trail if you are limiting your hiking weight is a goodly supply of space food sticks, raisins, or German chocolate bars. When you are lost in the woods in cold weather and are hungry, it really doesn't matter what you eat as long as you eat. Calorie energy input is a must because of the great drain on body reserves demanded by severe cold weather.

A lost snowshoer could look for animal tracks, snare and eat the animal if possible. The next best thing would be to see what the animal has been eating. The tips of spruce needles are edible. Wild apples can be cooked and eaten. Lichen from rocks can be simmered, steamed and beaten into a gruel. The taste is marginally horrible, but lichen is edible. The tops of cattails and the roots can be boiled and beaten into a gruel. Don't knock it until you have tried it. Such natural food could save your life.

Some additional tips on survival are listed below. Most of these are not vital, but will add to your comfort and well being.

1. Don't eat snow to quench thirst. Melting snow in your mouth uses up a considerable amount of body heat badly needed to sustain yourself. If you are thirsty, start a fire, and melt the snow in this way. Remember that your body needs water. It is best to start the day with a drink of water, have some water at midday, and some before you go to bed. Dehydration is a serious problem during the winter months. You notice the thirst demand less easily because the weather is cold.

2. Snow blindness as mentioned above is a hazard to be watched for [no pun intended]. The symptoms are a scratchness around the eyes, blurriness, and an inability to distinguish distant objects. The best cure for snow blindness is prevention. Buy and wear goggles or snow glasses. If however, you do become snow blind, you can shape a pair of goggles from a tree. Remove a strip of bark from a *dead* tree. The strip should be about four inches long and three inches wide. Cut a half-inch slit horizontally in the middle of the bark. Cut a place for your nose, and fasten them to your head by a piece of thong.

3. If you are travelling across lakes or are in the vicinity of open water, it is best to carry a pair of ice picks in your pocket. These picks can be made from a two inch piece of dowling. Cut the dowling to fit your hand, drill lead holes, and drive two nails through the wood. Sharpen the point of the nail, and put a piece of cork on the tip to prevent being stabbed by the point. These instruments come in very handy when you fall into water above your head. Carry the picks in an outer pocket where they can be easily reached in an emergency.

Commercial Model: Hand Rescue Ice Pick.

4. Before you venture forth into the wilderness buy several large garbage bags. Wrap all of the equipment in your duffle bag in these bags using different colored strings to tie the bags shut. Place all of the individually wrapped equipment into another large plastic bag, and slip this bag into your duffle. The procedure not only keeps all of your gear dry, but it makes for a neater pack. Remember the color of string you have for each kind of equipment, and you won't have to open each bag to find the thing you are looking for.

5. Ground to air emergency code.

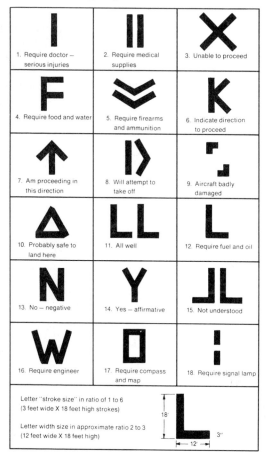

6. Sometime during snowshoeing, you are going to break a snowshoe. It is almost unavoidable because of the many obstructions encountered on trails. The plastic snowshoes do not break as easily, but they do break.

If you break a snowshoe, do not sit down and cry. Sit down and build yourself a new snowshoe. Brush snowshoes are simple to construct, and they will last long enough to get you out of the woods. The following method will produce one snowshoe. Since there is no right or left, make two or the going will be tough. This recipe for brush snowshoes comes from Herman Smith, the resource recreation agent at Rhinelander, Wisconsin.

Trimming the extra branches.

"Cut four or five green forked sticks, about the diameter of your thumb. Allow about four feet for each cut. Do not trim off any small branches or twigs. Lay one branch on top of the other and bind the pair of forks together, then twist each pair of parallel branches. Lay the bound forks opposing each other and bind the ends together. The framework is now constructed.

Three or four cross pieces must be bound across the main frame to support your foot. Make sure the center of balance is slightly to the rear. This enables the toe to rise when a step is

THE WHITE EARTH

Bind the branches together with heavy cord or wire.

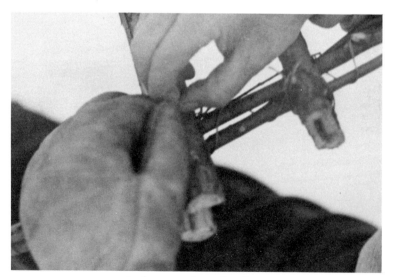

Lash cross pieces together.

made, otherwise the show point would dig into the snow at each step. Weave the fine twigs back and forth between the sides of the frame. Cut more twigs if necessary to lace in so your brush snowshoe will be more compact.

Bindings can be fashioned from any flexible material in an emergency, even strips of cloth torn from your shirttail. In practice, it would be best to use your leather belt of straps from your pack for binding materials.

Lace small branches into the frame to make the webbing.

THE WHITE EARTH

The completed brush snowshoe. This shoe will function long enough to get you out of the woods.

The completed brush snowshoe in use. The shoe is properly balanced with the toepiece lifting forward.

This is the law of the Yukon, that only
the strong shall thrive;
Then surely the weak shall perish, and
only the fit survive.

The Law of the Yukon
Robert William Service

Chapter Six

Getting Set

When Labor Day arrives in the north country it is as if a big hand quickly closes a curtain, calling an abrupt end to summer. It's that quick. Summer is over and so are many regular outside activities. The summer muscle tone eases away with less exercise which normal outdoor activity would promote.

Don't catch the Labor Day let-down. Snowshoers should maintain a proper exercise level all year around. The best way to exercise is to keep it fun. Stay away from boring routine exercises. However, even the fun exercises, if done day-after-day and week-after-week, risk becoming boring.

Try a variety of exercises. The following list includes activities which are good, tested ways to stay in shape before you snowshoe or participate in other winter activities. It's much like maintaining a spring training schedule all year around. In past years, baseball players would hit the banquet circuit after the final ball game in fall and report to spring training fat and round of shape. Today the smart ball player keeps in shape all year around. He watches what he eats on the banquet circuit, plus maintaining a moderate winter exercise schedule.

The prime example of the benefits of the come-to-camp-in-shape theory is Joe Torre of the New York *Mets*. Torre reported to the Cardinal training camp in 1971 thirty pounds lighter than his 1970 playing weight. All Joe did was pound the hide off of the ball during the 1971 season and was named the National League's most valuable player.

Proper exercise for winter activists should not be limited to snowshoers. Even the snowmobilers should maintain a regular exercise level. Many heart attacks have resulted among snowmobilers whose snow machines ran amuck deep in the woods. The trouble begins when, out of shape, they attempt to walk through the deep snow for help. It's tough going without snowshoes and deep snow could mean serious physical trouble—ending in fatal heart damage.

Push-Ups

A great exercise. It develops muscle tone similar to lifting weights. The one great advantage of the push-up over weights is that you don't have to lug the heavy weights around with you as you travel. You can always do push-ups, on the road or at home. Start with about ten push-ups and work your way up to your own natural capability and ability. You'll feel great. Gradually you will notice a new muscle tone to your entire body.

Jogging

Whether it's jogging outdoors or jogging indoors in place, you will find this exercise stimulating and one that builds endurance. The toughest part of this exercise is changing into jogging clothes and making the effort to put on your sneakers. Most of us feel it's a lot of trouble and not worth it. Bunk! Jogging becomes second nature after the first couple of weeks.

Touch Football

This is my sport. It should be labeled tough football for it is the best all around conditioner I have found. Even a game

Good physical exercise means that you can take all the punishment
winter has to give.

with three players on each side really gets the muscle tone up and keeps one in shape. A perfect game for the fall of the year. It's a fun exercise, great for building lung expansion and oxygen consumption.

Basketball

This is a great conditioner. Stay away from the half-court game. Full court is the only way to get the exercise benefit. You want muscle tone, not target awards. That comes from running and pacing your physical powers.

Hiking

I love a hike. Perhaps hikes were drummed into my skull when I was a Marine. I'll never forget those wonderful twelve mile hikes—packs and all. Our rest periods were always highlighted by an order to march in place while the other platoons sat on their duffs on the side of the road. Our drill instructor wanted us to be the best platoon in camp. Back in a normal world, hikes in the fall can be most stimulating. You might hike the same trail as you will during the winter. Notice the many changes in nature as the seasons swing. It will also familiarize you with the general lay of the land to help reduce that lost feeling that comes when the snow changes the scenery to white.

Handball or Paddleball

Perhaps the toughest of all conditioners. Quickness and stamina are what handball demands. Great physical toning is the reward for playing this gut-squeezing game. Be careful to pace yourself when beginning to play handball to avoid heart damage. Paddleball is a game similar to handball and not so tough on the body.

Exercise is the key. It really doesn't matter what exercise you do, just do something. You can do as much as you want or as little. But for your own sake, do something physical to keep life flowing through your body.

Whose woods these are I think I know.
His house is in the village though;
He will not see me stopping here
To watch his woods fill up with snow.

Stopping by the Woods on a Snowy Evening
Robert Frost

Chapter Seven

Walking On Snowshoes

Walking on snowshoes was best described by Bill Gilbert in the *Sports Illustrated* issue of Feb. 19, 1968:

"Snowshoeing . . . is a pleasure in and of itself. The pleasure is somewhat comparable to that of skin diving, sail-planing, or rubber rafting down a fast river. There is a sense of freely floating, drifting without much effort through a strange, rare world."

One of the advantages of learning how to snowshoe is that it doesn't take very long to become an accomplished snowshoer.

Most novice snowshoers can move about after about ten minutes. Be prepared to fall. You will fall many times on your first outing until you get the feel of that strange snowshoe on the bottom of your foot.

The so-called snowshoe experts I have researched in preparing this book often contradict each other when telling the snowshoe rookie how to take his first step. However, I have discarded their recommendations and offer the best advice yet: Don't fall down and don't put one snowshoe down on top of the other as you step out on the trail. If you do, you will take a spill. Experience is still the best teacher.

Novice snowshoe walking is a strange sensation. Keep your snowshoed feet far enough apart so you don't bang your ankles. Perhaps the best analogy of walking on snowshoes is that of walking in big, loose slippers.

The biggest problem in stepping out on snowshoes for the first-time is that of stepping on your other snowshoe.

Awkward falls are a part of snowshoeing.

You will be using calf and thigh muscles that you don't use in everyday walking. Go slow at first, is the word of caution. If you don't go slow at first you may suffer severe leg cramps.

The French-Canadian voyageurs, who tramped through snow-covered woods miles daily, called these leg pains *mal de raquette* which translates into "snowshoe sickness."

Although you must keep your legs apart, don't make it uncomfortable for yourself. A normal walking position is sufficient.

If you fall—it's no big deal! Don't take yourself too seriously. Work yourself back up on your feet. Trees and shrubs can be an aid to the fallen snowshoer. If nothing works as an

THE WHITE EARTH

aid in helping the fallen snowshoer, remove the bindings (an easy task) and then climb to your feet.

Turning

As mentioned earlier in Chapter One, the bearpaw-style snowshoes are the easiest for turning—in the woods or out on the snow trail. Their stubbiness eases the whole turning process in that they are less likely to snag. Use a clockwise motion if possible. A simple, broad turn is made as you move your right

Walking on the shoes.

snowshoe to the right slightly, followed with the left. Repeat these short movements until you are aimed in the direction you want to go.

When I first learned to ski, my instructor started me with the toughest turn of all—the kick turn. The kick turn looked impossible until I tried it. I lifted my right ski and plopped it 180 degrees to my rear. The left ski was still pointing ahead at this point and my right ski was pointed to the rear. It was a strange feeling for a novice skier. It's much easier to do than it sounds. It was a very simple matter to bring my left ski around so both skiis were now facing to what previously was my rear position. I might add that I was aided by my ski poles. However, the 180-degree kick turn can be accomplished on snowshoes with a little practice and it can be done without ski poles. Simply lift up your right leg and turn it 180 degrees to the rear. Follow with the left snowshoe and you're off.

This woodsman demonstrates the kick turn. He is in control of the snowshoe and not vice versa.

Climbing

The steepness of a hill should be your guide for the method to use in climbing the hill. If it is a moderate hill you can probably walk straight up the side. I have even seen some cross-country skiers walk straight up a moderate hill on their skiis.

Steeper hills require the traverse method. It's a zig-zag style which resembles sailing into the wind. If the hill is extremely steep, use the herringbone, or side step method. It is slower, but it works, and safely.

It is important that you learn how to edge your snowshoes when ascending. Edging means planting your snowshoe in the snow on the inside edge of each snowshoe. If you let it get away, so to speak, by stepping on the outside edge—be prepared for a tumble. Step down firmly on each step.

Make your presence felt on the snow. You will get the hang of it after a short while. Think inside edge when ascending for better control. You're after better stability.

Remember, play it by foot.

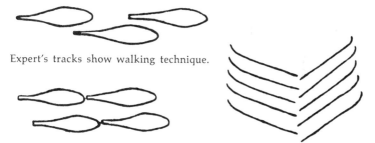

Expert's tracks show walking technique.

Beginners walk with uncomfortable waddle.   Herringbone climb tracks.

Snow Travel

Another fun aspect of snowshoeing is cross-country travel. Although I enjoy hitting a snow trail for exercise—going at a fast clip—it is the better part of valor to travel with a companion.

For picnic-type trips, small groups (4 to 6) are fun. It's surprising what a joint effort of doing something together, can do.

Sometime's the world's worst joke becomes funny in the fresh air. Hell, I even sang once on the trail. If you are going to picnic—don't overdo it. And always save some food for the return trip in case of an emergency.

And never venture from the lodge without emergency rations.

If someone was to suggest a race to the top of a rugged mountain and back to its base between a cross-country skier and

A downhill trek using modified bearpaws.

a snowshoer, here's my ten dollars on the tortoise-like snowshoer. The skier in all probability will give up or just won't make it. However, if the cross-country skier does have a little smarts, he will remove his skiis at difficult obstacles and that could make the race a little more interesting.

The snowshoer, for the most part, will seek an easier and faster route up the mountain. He will gain the race advantage up the hill. Down the hill, the snowshoer will gain an even greater advantage. Snowshoeing involves a movement similar to a shuffle or a slow jog. Anyone, fat and skinny alike, can use this jogging step on the snow trail and still not feel any great strain even after a mile. But don't get the impression that snowshoeing is like floating on heavenly clouds. It can be tiring.

Your walk on snowshoes will resemble the motions of an awkard duck. With each step the snowshoer will sink in the snow. It resembles walking up hill as the next step will be toward a new level of snow even though the snowshoer appears to be walking on level ground.

A snowshoe trail up and around a stand of birch trees.

This pretty snowshoer fires a fast snowball at the camera.

Nature is no sentimentalist—does not cosset or pamper us. We must see that the world is rough and surly.

Ralph Waldo Emerson

Chapter Eight

Winter Fun

In Emerson's manner we must seek our fun. Joy is another commodity. Winter fun is a whole new ball game. Not only does winter give you an outlet, but most winter fun activities are extremely healthful. I will tell you about some of the activities you can do with your snowshoes. If your favorite isn't listed, write to me and offer your own fun actions.

Picnic

There is nothing more pleasing after a day of tramping the trails on snowshoes than an old-fashioned picnic. It is similar to the shore lunch you've probably eaten after a day of fishing. You can make your meal as plain or as fancy as you desire. One friend garnishes his winter outdoor camp meal with New York strip steaks and a touch, just a touch, of red wine. Hot, boiled tea with sugar is always welcome for a cold picnic party.

Winter Fishing

No, people who fish in winter haven't gone off the deep end. Ice fishing is fun. Fish may be taken in winter by dark house spearing or caught through a hole in the ice with modified fishing gear. But check your state's fishing regulations to be safe and to be a good sportsman. I once did research for a newspaper feature story by following a game warden around during the winter in the Pewaukee, Wisconsin area. We tramped over lake after lake, checking on the gear used by the fisherman as well as checking for their licenses. The warden didn't miss much, not an ice cube was left unturned. The tip-up fish rig is used by most Wisconsin and Michigan ice fishermen. It's the lazy man's

Winter fishing in Wisconsin.

way of winter fishing. The tip-up usually has a flag attached to a small T-square kind of device with hook and line attached to the end of the T-arm. The rig is placed over the hole and when the fish hits, the flag is tipped up, signalling the fisherman to do something and do it quickly. You should check your state fish laws for use of tip-ups. If you are going to snowshoe—winter fish, your hole should be chopped near the middle of the lake or over a deep spot. Bait is not a real problem for fish in winter will almost strike at anything. I've even seen a small piece of shiny tin can attached to a hook as a bait and it worked perfectly. If you don't have any live bait, a small piece of brightly-colored cloth or yarn can be used.

During cold weather, the water in your hole may freeze over. The freezing slush must be removed from the hole. If you don't have a standard ice scoop sold for such purpose, then improvise. Get a free twig from the shore and stir the water once in a while to keep the slush from setting into ice. Covering the hole with some brush will help keep the hole from freezing but it plays hob with the operation of the tip-up. Some fishermen use a coffee can which contains a few lumps of glowing charcoal. This hot can is floated in the water of the open hole, and, of course, keeps the ice from freezing the fishing hole shut.

Racing

As mentioned earlier, the so-called world record for the 100-yard dash on snowshoes is 12.2 seconds. And that's pretty quick. If you don't think so, try it. A race may be set up for varying distances similar to the standard summer track and field events —the 100, 220, and the 440 yard dashes. Additional can be the

Snowshoe racers on a snow track.

880 yard which was very popular with my Drill Instructor in the Marines, the mile, and even a five-mile event. The length of a race you might enter depends on your conditioning and capability. Racing is a good event for an outdoor sportsman's club to sponsor. Some energetic Jaycee group in the north country could sponsor the races for some charity or for the repair of those injured in their community as a result of snowmobile accidents. The local newspaper in Minocqua, *The Lakeland Times*, each week during winter reports an occasional tragic snowmobile injury. It would be a worthy project to help the families of those who are burdened with large medical bills. The benefits from the race would not be limited to snowmobile cases, but include those injured in skiing accidents and all winter-related misfortunes.

Records: International Snowshoe Race

Event	Winning time
100-yard dash	12.1 seconds
220-yard dash	25.6 seconds
440-yard run	68.7 seconds
880-yard run	2:49.0 minutes*
1 mile	5:18.6 minutes

* In the Marine Corps, the 880-yard run was known as the old walnut-breaker.

Snowshoe Baseball

Play the game the regular way. Bases should be spaced about 40 feet apart—distance from home to first and from home to third. The trouble with getting up a winter ball game is the recruiting of enough snowshoe enthusiasts to have two complete teams. It is fun, and if played with a 12-inch softball or the big 16-inch mushball, it gets to be a riot once the ball becomes frozen or water-logged.

Snowshoe baseball also is played in summer, believe it or not! The game I am familiar with is played at Lake Tomahawk, Wisconsin. It is a fun spectator sport and a real muscle test for the participants. Lake Tomahawk does the game up big during the summer by inviting the Rhinelander, Wisconsin's crack girl drill team "The Belles of St. Mary" to entertain the tourists. It's a town fun night during the summer. Tourists are the royalty of northern summers—even the town bankers smile at the outlanders!

Snowshoe softball.

Tough Football

Tough is right. It's not touch football. Somewhere along the line somebody forgot to tell the touch football players that you don't beat the hell out of your opponent. But playing tough football on snowshoes is another ball game—taken literally. Try running for a pass on snowshoes, much less playing a whole game. The aches and pains the next day will give you the clue that you really do have unused muscles—like a zillion. I've played college football with pads and the works. I've also played tough football. Without a doubt, I label tough football as the roughest. Played without pads or any protection, taking an elbow in the chops while snowshoeing at full speed is not a thrilling moment. Our Chicago *Tribune* Sunday morning league games used to be quite combative. Channel 5, WMAQ-TV, would use their star sports announcer, Johnny Morris, who is an ex-Bear. He's the only player I've ever seen in tough football who ran for a 95-yard touchdown, and it wasn't a pass.

Catch

Tossing a ball back and forth can be fun on snowshoes. It seems simple, and it is. However, a long, wrong reach means snow on your fanny as you tumble.

Obstacle Races

Set up a series of hurdles or use natural ones—fallen trees, small snow drifts. And then race against a clock, each contestant

taking turns. Try for the best time over the course. Good for laughs, and a day of complete exhaustion!

Snowshoe Hockey

Snowshoe hockey is ideally played on an open, frozen lake with a surface of hard crust. Set up the goals using twigs or branches. Use a 12-inch softball as a puck. If you really want to have a fun game, try to beat a football through the snow with a hockey stick. You can never be sure where your slap shot might be headed. The game can be played with or without a goalie, since it won't make much difference in the final score.

Dodge Ball

Played on snowshoes, this game takes on a new fun similar to the dodge ball played by school kids on a playground. Establish boundaries and then with a volleyball, or any large, soft ball for that matter, attempt to hit an opponent. Remember, only three steps can be taken by the person throwing the ball. The lone survivor is the grand winner.

Biathlon

This strange sport consists of firearms skill plus cross-country skiing or snowshoeing race over a predetermined course during which a stop is made to shoot at targets for score. Believe it or not, the biathlon is an Olympic sport. Perhaps you saw this Olympic contest on NBC from Sapporo, Japan. In my book, this race has no place in the Olympics. However, as a winter activity, especially for the snowshoer, it does have some merit. A course is again prepared with the turn-around a prepared target area. The snowshoer tramps out to the target area and fires at a target for score and then heads back to the finish line in a race against the clock. Best time and best target scores are tabulated the same way as the Olympic biathlon. Shots which miss count as deductions from the total time of the individual snowshoer.

Follow the Leader

A clever leader can set a fun pace for the snowshoe pack. Show-off snowshoe tricks like a 180° jump turn in the air or walking backwards on snowshoes can provide a barrel of laughs.

Snowshoe Safari

Jim Maines, a science teacher at North Lakeland Elementary School in Minocqua, Wisconsin, organized a Valentine's Day snowshoe safari recently. One amazing thing he discovered, according to Mary B. Good, a former reporter for the *Lakeland Times*, was that many of the youngsters who participated in the safari had never been into the woods on foot during winter. This was in northern Wisconsin!

Maines invited 100 enthusiastic kids along on his annual trek through the woods on snowshoes. Mary Good wrote that it looked like a "convention of robots" walking stiffly through the brush.

A playful dog adds to the enjoyment of a snow walk. Note the different outfits the snowshoers wear.

She also reported that the snowshoers took many spills, while snowballs were being exchanged as airborne "gifts." Horseplay and good fun, however, was all part of the day. Afterwards, the tired kids enjoyed a chocolate and cookie break back at the school.

Snowshoe sport clubs are very much alive and well. The snowshoe clubs of Canada and America are very active in aiding the tremendous and exciting rebirth of a once-dying sport.

The Inter-Collegiate Winter Sports Union has given official status to snowshoeing. The International Snowshoe Congress is the governing body which controls competitive events.

Experts can walk for hours on snowshoes at a rate of six miles per hour, according to naturalist Ben Thoma, writing in the *Conservation Volunteer*. Beginners need considerable time and experience to be able to sustain this distance-hour rate. Short distances, Thoma writes, can be covered at a dogtrot of about ten miles per hour! Who can guess the calorie-per-hour fuel expenditure needed for this speed? It is no wonder that plenty of trail snacks are needed.

There are many games that can be played on snowshoes. Test your imagination. Think of a few new ones. Readers who do think of some more fun games on snowshoes are encouraged to send them to me. Better yet, tell others about your variations and let me hear of the new games by the grapevine. Form snow shoe clubs so that you will have a group large enough to undertake this list of winter games. It's also good to have someone with whom you can share your aches and pains.

Whitetail deer. It is rare that snowshoers will get this close to the animals.

Snowshoe tennis anyone?

"History is bunk."

Henry Ford
in witness box during libel
suit vs. *The Chicago Tribune*
July, 1919

Chapter Nine

Snowshoe History

The discovery of snowshoes probably happened accidentally much like the discovery of fire.

Likely, it was a very cold day with the snow blowing horizontally across the cave opening. Joe Caveman was sitting in his cave enjoying a warm fire and all the comforts of a cave home on a cold winter's night. Cavewoman, however, wasn't content at seeing her mate rest while she dusted the rock furniture.

"Get out of the house you big lug," she yelled sweetly. "Go get some yak meat for tonight's orgy."

"But the snow is up to my belly button," the disgruntled mate replied.

With that cavewoman, a docile, liberated Amazon, picked up a frying rock and tossed it at caveman. It bounced off his skull, landing outside the cave on the snow. She grabbed another frying rock and flung it after her fleeing cavemate. It again zonked him on the noggin, landing at his feet. His one foot landed in the first pan. Caveman discovered that his "panned" foot did not sink in the snow like his "unpanned" foot. He picked up the other pan and placed it under his other foot.

Not only did it help the caveman maneuver better in the snow, but it also helped him wander away from the old bat back at the cave. He snowpanned his way all the way to the palms of Fort Cavedale, Florida, where he opened the first successful dino-burger franchise while freelancing as a pictographer for *Caveboy* magazine.

Anthropologists generally believe that the snowshoe was developed in north-central Asia about 5,000 years ago. The exact date would be impossible to pinpoint. It is enough to know that man can adapt to any climatic condition when pressed by the need to expand his life support range. The use of snowshoes spread in both directions toward the subpolar regions. Leaving large print trails like a wandering Yeti, the use of snowshoes spread throughout the cold lands of Europe and North America. In North America, the Indians undertook the further refinement of the snowshoe.

However, traces of a snowshoe or a ski-type of foot attachment have been found in European Stone and Bronze age excavations. These snowshoe artifacts have been discovered in the bogs and marshes of Norway, Finland, Sweden, and Russia. The snowshoe was used in Finland and Sweden as long ago as 4,500 to 5,000 years. At Umea, Sweden, about 4,500 years ago the "Hoting" ski was invented. Some 2,500 years ago in the south of Norway the "Ovrebo" ski was in use. The Ovrebo had a turned-up front and was somewhat pointed—an improvement on the snowshoe. In the *Sagas*, the classic hero tales of the Vikings, reference is made to the use of snowshoes about 1000 A.D.

The first mention of skiis or snowshoes being used in war-time was during the Norwegian Civil War, 1206. King Sverre sent two scouts, called "Birchlegs"—they wrapped their legs in birch bark as protection against the cold—to carry the royal infant son, Haakon Haakonson over the mountains to safety.

Today in Norway the annual *Birkebinerrennet* (birch leg race) is held as a cross-country event. The birch leg race follows the

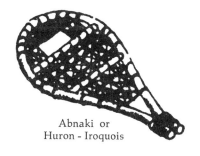

Abnaki or
Huron - Iroquois

Salish or
Bearpaw

Above, Athapaskan, round toe
and, below, Athapaskan, pointed toe.

Naskapi
two-piece frame

Wooden snowshoe
(for melting snow)

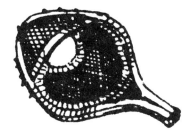

same 35-mile course covered by King Sverre's scouts, some 750 years ago.

In 1521 Swedish King Gustav Vasa fled his land on snowshoes to safety in Norway. Overtaken by his own men and persuaded to return and fight the invading Danes, King Gustav snowshoed back and led his Swedes to victory.

The *Vasaloppet* race held in Sweden today follows the original route in a national celebration of King Gustav's victory over the Danes.

It seems strange, but the people who likely needed snowshoes the most, the Eskimos, were the last peoples to adopt them. Actually, Eskimos had little need for the snowshoe since they are mostly aquatic hunters, traveling over hard-packed snow and ice.

Without the snowshoe, it is doubtful whether man could have migrated to colder climates. Winter survival in the deep snow country would have been impossible without the ability to hunt and travel on snowshoes.

The Laplanders are also included in an early history of the snowshoe culture. The Athapascan Indians of the North American

One reindeer power sled.

plains and Canadian west coast, and the Algonquin Indians of the Ottawa and St. Lawrence river valleys almost perfected the bearpaw-style snowshoe.

THE WHITE EARTH

The Plains Indians often used snowshoes to help them during the buffalo hunt. They realized their dependence on the snowshoe. In anticipation of fierce winters, they had a special ceremonial dance prior to the first great snow.

Although the Indians were using snowshoes by 1000 A.D., explorer Leif Ericson did not report seeing Indians using snowshoes. In all probability Ericson didn't see anything unusual about the Indians using snowshoes and thus failed to record it.

The French adopted the Indian snowshoe in the St. Lawrence River area in the early 1600's. In fact, the smart French woodsmen probably used the snowshoe to great advantage in their battles against the British for control of the North American fur trade and land.

Not only did man use the snowshoe to his advantage in maneuvering in snow country, but an early 16th-century woodcut shows a mountaineer and a pack horse both sporting round snowshoes!

Sled dogs and snowshoes. The most common means of transportation in the northland during the winter.

A 96'er hitting the Yukon trail.

There is no fundamental difference between man
and the higher animals in their mental faculties.

From the DESCENT OF MAN
Charles Darwin

Chapter Ten

Animal Tracks

Animal tracks in the snow can prove to be a winter adventure all in itself for the snowshoer. The silent world was once
attributed to underwater life and the plethora of adventure that
went along with its exploration. There is another silent world
—the northern woods in winter. If you can find the sounds of
silence which are very loud, you will find a moment of peace,
beauty, and truth in nature.

Perhaps the most common tracks found in the woods are
those of the deer. They are easy to recognize and easy to find.
Deer will follow any trail in the snow so if your snowshoe route
is a regular one through the woods, in all probability you will
find deer tracks there too.

Winter animals are able to change their body insulation
according to the needs of the particular situation. The Arctic Fox,

for instance, does not need to produce extra heat until the temperature falls below 40° below zero. All wintering animals shed their thick undercoats in summer so the heat does not bother them. Animals which live in cold places usually have shorter ears, limbs, and tails than their relatives in warmer climates. The shorter ears, limbs, and tails reduce the body surface area through which body heat can be lost.

Animals lose very little heat through their limbs because they have a system of counter-current that conserves the heat in the central body mass. Less energy is required to keep their proper body temperatures, and snow does not melt on their legs and feet because these are usually colder than the body. If water were to melt on their legs and then form into ice, the animals would soon become bogged down by the weight of the ice on their legs. So in a sense they are protected by nature from the elements, but not from man.

Deer tracks measure from 2 to 3 inches in length and are about 25 inches apart when the deer is walking a straight line.

Whitetail Deer
Identification: White tail or flag and antlers which do not branch and rebranch. Only male develops antlers and are worn only a limited time each year.
Food: In winter, forced to eat cedar, briars, balsam, and spruce along with dead leaves and dead grass.

Grizzly Bear
Identification: Black to light cream. King of the North American game animals. Typical male weighs 500 pounds. Poor vision, but excellent smell and hearing.
Food: Green grass, rock-chucks, mice, gophers, roots, nuts, berries and especially the bears like fish.

THE WHITE EARTH

Fisher

Identification: More powerful, darker in color than a martin. About 3 feet in length.

Food: Small mammals and birds with few nuts and berries when other food is scarce. Adept at killing the porcupine without getting full of quills. Rips the underside of its victim with sharp claws.

Moose

Identification: Largest game animal in North America. Bell, bag of skin with long hair, which hangs from the jaw. Bull and cow dark brown in color. Big bulls can weigh 1800 pounds.

Food: Depends heavily on willow browse in winter.

Alaskan Brown Bear

Identification: Average weight of 800 pounds. Unpredictable behavior as characteristic of bears. Fighting speed is tremendous.

Food: Vegetable diet is abandoned when the salmon start to run.

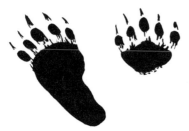

Polar Bear
Identification: Large males often weigh 1500 to 1600 pounds. Fur white in winter, yellowish in summer.
Food: The seal, but will turn to fish, porpoise, whale, roots, seaweed, grass, ducks and scoters.

Otter
Identification: Feet webbed. Member of weasel family. Long lithe body, short legs, and heavy tail. Good swimmer.
Food: Crayfish, fish, muskrats, young beavers, ducks, poultry, and frogs.

Wolverine
Identification: Largest and most fierce of the weasel family. Male about 36 inches in length; weight, 25 pounds.
Food: Kills other animals. Steals bait from hunter's traps. Mainly a meat eater.

THE WHITE EARTH

Badger

Identification: Short, stout legs, and a thick heavy body. About 28 inches long. Paws have sharp claws. Head is black with a white stripe on back.

Food: Captures his prey by digging them out of their dens. Gophers, prairie dogs, and ground squirrels. Also mice, insects, roots and young birds.

Black Bear

Identification: A black bear may be anything but black although black is predominant. Average weight 200 to 500 pounds. Occasional white patch on the breast.

Food: Inclined to be a vegetarian. Root and berry eater, but will change to meat. Grass, fruit, berries, grubs, insects, fish, carrion, and fresh meat.

Martin

Identification: Member of weasel family. Body slightly smaller than common house cat. Medium-short bushy tail. Head is small, ears are broad. Pelt valuable.

Food: Squirrels, small rodents, mice, chipmunks, and rabbits. Grouse and other birds. Few reptiles, frogs and insects. Nuts, fruits and berries.

Bobcat

Identification: Somewhat smaller than the Canadian lynx. Tail slightly longer. Tufts on ears not so pronounced. Tawny brown with dark brown spots on back and sides. Underparts are yellowish-white spotted with black. Weight 20 to 25 pounds.

Food: Small game, small rodents, fawns, birds. Especially fond of young wild turkeys. Lambs in sheep country; small pigs and poultry.

Canadian Lynx

Identification: Awkward appearing cat with long legs. Very short tail, large paws and long tufts on ears. Tail tipped with black. Color is soft, warm gray. Sometimes with brownish patches. Males sometimes 40 pounds.

Food: Venison, birds. Similar to bobcat.

Wolves

Identification: Gray tends to be heavier in the northern range than the red. Large wolves weigh 175 pounds.

Food: Musk ox to mice. Preys on the sick animals in deer herds, moose and caribou herds.

Coyote

Identification: Adult will weigh about 21 pounds and the length is 4 feet, including the tail. Similar to German shepherd in appearance. However, dog is his mortal enemy. Color somewhat lighter than in summer.

Food: Birds, insects, carrion, rabbits, poultry and sheep. Packs can kill animals of deer size.

Fox

Red and grey fox differ in appearance and habitat. Red fox weighs about 9 pounds and the grey about 7 pounds. Have same number of teeth as dogs.

Food: Field mice, rabbits, birds, poultry, insects, fruit, berries, snakes and crayfish.

Rabbit

Identification: Average weight of 2 to 3 pounds. Timid and easily frightened.

Food: Herbs in summer, short shrubs and clover. Bark and twigs in winter.

Grey Squirrel
Identification: Weight about 1 pound. Measures 19 inches in length, 9 inches of which is tail.
Food: Nuts, buds, corn and apples.

Woodchuck
Identification: Commonly called the groundhog. Two feet in length; legs are short and body is solidly built. True hibernator.
Food: Diet is limited to vegetation.

GAME TRACKING IN WINTER

Nature's greatest thrill is the thrill of discovery—and it's yours for the asking! No admission charge. No equipment needed. Not even a license required. You need not travel far, either, for the closest woodlot or small stream with wooded banks will do. You will find an abundance of wildlife living within traffic sound of our largest cities.

A clear, calm day after a light snow will provide plenty of trails. However, don't be content merely to identify a track, but follow it for some distance. Notice the changes in pace as shown

THE WHITE EARTH

by the distance between leaps or steps. Try to determine the reason. Other nearby tracks may help. Perhaps this furry friend of ours was a hunter—or the hunted! Food habits, droppings and dens all tell an intriguing story. Traits which have no apparent reason but are peculiar to certain animals may be discovered.

The sportsman who is a hunter can spend time during the off-season learning more of the game of his choice. The successful trapper has spent many hours following trails, learning the habits and locations of the fur-bearers he hopes to trap. He considers this a pleasant and important part of his work.

There is, perhaps, no better way to introduce a youngster to nature than on a walk in search of snow trails. Young and old will find that nature reveals many of her secrets in winter that are difficult, if not impossible, to solve at any other time.

Courtesy: *Pennsylvania Game News*
By Clyde L. Allison
Outdoor Photographers League

Day-old rabbit tracks. Note the edges of the tracks have melted, and are fuzzy.

Chapter Eleven

The Snowmobile

Before I speak out against the snowmobile, I must confess
that at one time I loved the snowmobile. There was nothing that
was more fun than to run at full throttle across a frozen lake
in Vilas County. It was a thrill. The speed—the wind in my
face—the excitement of the moment, it was all there!

Then the reports of deaths and of maiming injuries started
filtering across the news desk at the *Tribune*.

Even the bars I visited around the Minocqua area displayed
posters proclaiming a benefit, or some public affair to raise funds
for a local snowmobiler who had been seriously injured when
his snowmobile crashed.

One such snowmobile accident, a source in Minocqua told
me, occurred when the 24-year-old snowmobiler, who was going

about 60 miles an hour, hit a slick patch at the side of the road and crashed into an icy snowbank!

The next week in northern Wisconsin there were "Benefit for Jim" posters spread throughout the Minocqua-Woodruff area. I am not knocking local community spirit in supporting these benefits. I think it is terrific that a town would lend support

Blindfolded children participating in a snowmobile race.

to such "in-need" victims. But I do protest the senseless snowmobile accidents that are turning snowmobiling into a kind of Russian roulette.

Cost

The snowmobile is expensive. The machines cost from between $600 to $2500 and weigh from 215 to 650 pounds.

Growth

The snowmobile made its commercial debut through Canada's Bombardier, Ltd., in 1959 (when 259 vehicles were sold). Today sales of snowmobiles has surpassed the one million figure in North America alone and sales are growing.

What started out as an adjunct to outboard motor sales has exceeded all expectations.

THE WHITE EARTH

Noise

"Let's face it, a cruise through the snow-shrouded pines under the light of a full moon is an experience you don't soon forget," a snowmobile proponent once stated. However, I'm sure Robert Frost had other ideas about the beauty and quiet of a snow-draped woods.

Snowmobiles are no worse than motorcycles. Their whines are piercing on a cold day. Michigan requires a muffler "in good working order" to prevent excessive or unusual noise and annoying smoke."

During my thrill days on a snowmobile, I remember once when I was zipping across a frozen lake in Oneida County, Wisconsin, on a snowmobile when the muffler failed. I honestly thought I was going to go deaf! I tried holding one hand over

A snowmobile moving across a frozen lake at 35 miles per hour.

my ear but still the terrible noise penetrated. After I got back to shore and turned the snowmobile back to the gentleman who let me use it, it was something like two hours before I could hear a conservation in a normal tone of voice.

The International Snowmobile Industry Association in a positive step has filed the following report:

As to snowmobiles, we have asked our members to test the noise levels on their various models, or have them

SNOWSHOE GUIDE BOOK

so checked, according to a uniform procedure which we selected. Each manufacturer keeps his own records and they are not reported to this office or tabulated. We did this so that our members will know what noise levels their machines are generating and put us in a position at any time to comment on any proposed noise level that might be considered on snowmobiles.

Letter from Harold Howe, Executive
Secretary, International Snowmobile
Industry Association, Nov. 21, 1968

From all the noise caused by the environmentalists concerning the raucous snowmobiles, perhaps the snowmobile industry is on the verge of waking up and designing quieter snowmobiles.

The Adirondack Mountain Club of New York State has proposed a realistic noise standard for snowmobiles. They propose that the operation in the state of off-road vehicles (ATV and motorcycles included) producing sounds (not only engine noise) be regulated at 73 decibels on the "A" scale at 50 feet.

Resource Damage

The snowmobile has been credited with damage to tree seedlings and golf courses. In the winter of 1969-70, northern New Hampshire tree farms reported snowmobile damage to some 30,000 young trees.

The state of Michigan and Minnesota prohibit snowmobile operation in nursery or other planting areas, according to Malcolm F. Baldwin in his book *The Off-Road Vehicle and Environmental Quality*. Additionally:

We have no detrimental environmental effects from snowmobiles with respect to wildlife, trails, noise, or trespass. On the contrary, snowmobile trails through the deep snow last winter were responsible for preservation of the deer herds in the parks.

Effects on Fish and Wildlife Population
Letter from R. W. Ertresvaag, deputy
director, North Dakota Park Service.

Snowmobiles are causing serious problems—Wildlife is frequently harassed and actually killed by snowmobiles pursuing them until they die of exhaustion. Damage to trees, fences and trails and general abuse of private land-

THE WHITE EARTH

owner's property are other problems frequently related to snowmobiling activities.

Letter from Oris J. Scherschlight, chief division of parks and recreation, South Dakota Department of Game Fish & Parks

Game harassment reports are common. There have been hunting abuses too numerous to mention. Such game harassment, specifically, the running down of deer, fox, coyote, and other animals have been reported in Alberta, Saskatchewan, the Yukon, Michigan and Minnesota.

Baldwin added, in his book, that the effective way to protect fish and wildlife from off-road vehicle effects is not by restricting hunting or harassment alone, but by *banning* these vehicles from important game habitat areas.

Theft and Vandalism

Cabins hidden away deep in so-called secluded areas are now vulnerable to burglary with the advent of the snowmobile. The snowmobile has made it easy for the dishonest person to peacefully loot a cabin hidden in some remote place. One of the policing and control tools being instigated to combat the snowmobile burglary of cabins is an identification device on snowmobilies. Large numerals and code letter should be required to be displayed on snowmobiles in every state. This identification registry will aid witnesses and law enforcement officials in their efforts to control cabin thievery.

The snowmobile owner should also welcome snowmobile registration as it would aid in the recovery of a stolen snowmobile.

France and Norway, two countries where the winter thing is king, have banned the snowmobile for pleasure use. Snowmobile use is only permissible in emergency situations and where other forms of travel in the snow are impossible.

Trespass

Sign companies that make "no trespassing" warnings are making money in northern Wisconsin. Anti-snowmobile landowners are posting their land in order to preserve it from trespass by the snowmobile pack. Broken fences, damaged crops and shrubbery are becoming commonplace, especially when an unwanted snowmobiler trespasses when the spring snow has all but melted.

If you are a landowner and you give permission to a snowmobile pack to romp on your land, please check your insurance in case one grateful snowmobiler has an accident on your land and decides to sue you. Check your liability clause. It could save you many headaches in the future.

Snowmobile Psychology

David Klein, a social science professor at Michigan State University, in a recent issue of *Journal of Safety Research* made a generalization about snowmobile fans: "They court danger to achieve satisfactions that their dull jobs cannot provide."

Klein says the problem stems from the discrepancy between cultural values and reality. In the United States, which is a highly industrialized nation, man has a tough time winning a pat on the back for doing his job. He compensates by surrounding him-

Snowmobile tracks leave their marks on the embankment of a road.

self with snowmobiles, power tools, super cars, and outboard motors. Klein says they give him, at play, "the feelings of control, power, masculinity, and risk no longer available at work."

The need to live dangerously is demonstrated by those who use snowmobiles. It is my opinion that the weekly reports of deaths and maiming injuries add to the danger involvement of those persons who get their thrills on snowmobiles.

"Americans do not want as safe an environment as could be achieved," according to Klein. "If an individual seeks risks, incorporation of safeguards into a recreational device is likely to send him in search of a less safe device."

If Klein's theory proves true and the snowmobile is slapped with heavy regulations, then look for the power-seeking sports enthusiast to seek his winter thrills in more daring ways.

Super powered ice skates capable to speeds up to 100 miles an hour? It could be an alternative if the snowmobile is too heavily regulated. The whine of the snowmobile is gradually replacing the raucous barks of huskies pulling dog sleds in Alaska and the north country. That's "progress" and it is a fact of life that the snowmobile is here to stay.

The economic impact in the northern areas of the country alone merits the further development and use of the snowmobile. There are definite misuses of the snowmobile by a few helmeted boobs. Fortunately, it is only a few snowmobilers who are creating a bad name for the sport.

The snowmobile as a rescue machine in the north is another plus for the whining machine. It has proved invaluable as a rescue vehicle in getting to difficult places in the snow country to give help.

Snowshoes, however, are a must for snowmobiles, especially near spring when the slush covers the frozen lakes. Walking in the lake slush is a hazard in itself.

If you can afford it, invest in two sets of snowshoes. A smaller model like the modified bearpaw snowshoe to use when the snow is up to ten inches deep; the other pair of snowshoes that would complete the snowshoer's foot gear is a trail model snowshoe similar to the Maine or Michigan model. The Maine or Michigans are excellent for snow over ten inches deep.

The bearpaws, although good in the woods and in shallow snow, are something less than wonderful for use in the deep snow.

Snowshoers and snowmobilers get together for some hot coffee.

"A loaf of bread, a juq of wine and thou."

From OMAR KHAYYAM
Edward Fitzgerald

Chapter Twelve

Winter Tales

BOOZE IN WINTER

I'm sure you have seen a picture of a St. Bernard dog with a small cask around its neck bringing comfort and relief in the form of a nip for some person stranded in the snow.

However, before you think of carrying a wine or whiskey flask with you to ward off the cold while snowshoeing, think it over.

Dr. Theodore Van Dellen, the Chicago *Tribune's* expert on medicine, rules against booze in the cold.

"Whiskey dilates the capillaries of the skin leading to a temporary sense of warmth," Dr. Van Dellen told me.

"Additional booze makes the individual numb or indifferent to the cold. It is here he may get into trouble. He perspires profusely, which is an excellent measure when it is hot. This is not advisable when it is cold, because there is a loss of body heat."

Your main concern in the cold is to maintain body heat. So drinking booze is not such a good idea on the snowshoe trail after all. However, when the day is ended and you are in front of that crackling fireplace, it's a whole new ball game.

FIELD NOTES

Make notes and dates of your snowshoe outings.

Date   Activity

Joy is not in things; it is in us.

Wagner

Winter is a beautiful thing. Winter is a treacherous thing. Tales of the wilderness have always fascinated me. Whether it is a wolf or a man braving the fierce elements of an Alaskan winter it doesn't matter. Both are in a life and death struggle against nature at her harshest moment.

Jack London was the foremost writer of the north. In his "The Call of The Wild" first published in 1903, London told about the reversion of a tamed dog to the savage state. Perhaps it was the truthful harshness of his stories that fascinated me.

One of the most poignant stories of the struggle against nature appeared in the Chicago *Tribune* and other newspapers recently. The headline read: Trapper's Dream Fades After Arctic Kills Wife.

The entire story is printed here thanks to the Associated Press.

FAIRBANKS, Alaska, March 18, 1972 — Mike Holland — broke and becoming discouraged — is a widower at age 29.

Faded is his dream of a peaceful but primitive life with his wife and infant son in a remote Yukon River trapper's cabin, far from the cities, crowds, and the comforts of technology.

His 21-year-old wife was slain by the harsh environment above the Arctic Circle, where they planned to stay because they liked it.

They lived alone in a tiny log cabin, subsisting mostly off the land, without electricity or communications with the outside world.

Their experiences were reported early this year in an Associated Press story which brought them hundreds of letters and gifts from all parts of the United States.

Disaster struck Feb. 15 when Sue Holland froze to death less than a mile from her home.

"I tried to tell people that this country can kill you, but they didn't understand," Holland said this week in Fairbanks, where he is trying to pick up the pieces of his life.

Mrs. Holland was near the end of a 30-mile snow machine trip from the tiny Indian community of Stevens Village.

Authorities said the woman's snow machine malfunctioned about halfway to the cabin. With overnight temperatures dipping to 45 degrees below zero, she set out on foot, leaving her survival gear and then shedding her snow shoes, before collapsing.

Sought Clues to Tragedy

Holland, who was waiting at the cabin, later went over her trail in an attempt to answer the question that accompanies tragedy.

"She didn't take the survival gear out of the snow machine," he said. "This is all supposition, but it indicated to me that she thought she could make the 14 miles without any difficulty at all.

"It was a case of being oversure of yourself in a country that will kill you in a moment if it can."

Mrs. Holland, a native of Havertown, Pa., was buried in a simple funeral at Stevens Village.

"Must Go Back"

Holland, who is from Alabama, said he must return to the Yukon River because trapping "is the only thing I know."

"Financially, I can't stay in Fairbanks," he said. "It's out there that I can live, I can feed myself. Here I can't. I have to go back."

Holland says he still must "straighten things out in my mind." But, tentatively, he hopes to take his infant son, now staying with friends in Fairbanks, to Stevens Village. There, he says, he will build a cabin in which to raise his son, and continue trapping near the now-lonely cabin further north.

"My main concern now," he says, "is for the baby."

Mike and Sue Holland with dogs Finny (rear) and Tess in their artic cabin.

THE WHITE EARTH

Angel on Snowshoes

A story about snowshoes would be incomplete if it omitted a mention of the "Angel on Snowshoes," Dr. Kate Newcomb of Woodruff, Wisconsin.

Dr. Kate often tramped through the north woods of Wisconsin, black bag in hand, to aid those who were in need of her services—day or night.

Although "her hospital in Woodruff is named Howard Young Medical Center, tourists and natives alike still refer to it as "Dr. Kate's Hospital."

Tales of Dr. Kate on snowshoes traveling over the snow at 40 degrees below zero in order to help a sick person are common and too numerous to mention.

Ralph Edwards heard of her exploits in California in 1954 and honored her on his "This Is Your Life" program. Edwards suggested to viewers that they might help her hospital open debt free. His single remark brought outstanding results.

In 1954 Woodruff, a town of 474, usually received one sack of mail a day. That week 274 pouches of mail arrived—all for Dr. Kate. The sum included 1,325,000 pennies and the hospital opened debt free.

Dr. Kate was a graduate from the University of Buffalo. She interned in a New York City hospital and later worked in a slum area there. Then she moved to Detroit where she married Bill Newcomb, an auto plant worker.

The Newcombs headed for the northwoods in 1923 because of Bill's failing health. They settled in a back trail cabin along the Rice river near Boulder Junction.

Dr. Kate put her medical practice aside as she claimed she was a "bit sour" on it after losing her first child. She had thoughts that she couldn't resume her medical practice in this "strange new world."

Then in 1931, Dr. Thomas Torpy of Minocqua, telephoned Dr. Kate and told her to handle an emergency case he could not take. She picked up her dusty medical bag and was back in business again.

On May 30th, 1956 Dr. Kate died after undergoing surgery to correct a broken hip. She was 69. Dr. Kate had slipped on wet pavement as she left a meeting at Lac du Flambeau school.

Dr. Kate Newcomb on showshoes heads out to help someone in need of her services.

THE WHITE EARTH

Funds in her name are still appreciated at Lakeland Hospital.

Dr. Kate's Christmas motto which decorated her home is worth remembering:

Pile on more wood
The wind is chill
But let it whistle
As it will.
We'll keep our Christmas
Merry still.

The Rev. J. P. Tanguay of the Immaculate Heart of Mary church at Teslin, Yukon offers the following piece about life on snowshoes in a northern winter.

The Longest Day

We were on our way across country from Prophet River to Fonts in northern British Columbia, some twenty years ago. The snow was three feet deep and deeper near the Sikanni River. With our snowshoes, we cleared a place to set our overnight camp but, we did not dare a step out of the area without our snowshoes.

Sipping our last cup of tea before retiring, Jumbie my Indian companion and I, were planning for the next day. "We have only some ten miles to get to Fontas, if Eddie Needley trapped in this direction, we should hit his trail soon; with an early start we should reach Fontas by evening." Our provisions were getting low, we had better keep moving. "I will be up at first daylight," I said, "good night."

Twenty below was quite comfortable in our snug and well-sheltered camp. At the crack of dawn, I was up and going through the morning ritual after a night in the open. I shook the embers, pulled the burning logs together, put on an armful of dry boughs and a couple of big logs. An invigorating heat filled the air; after a few slow spins, I was back to body temperature. I filled the tea pail with crystallized snow, hung it on the green willow over the fire, added more snow for good measure; when the lid danced to greet the boiling water, I dropped in a handful of coffee, allowed the extra boil for strength, covered the pail and set it in the ashes near the fire where, in the meantime, I had placed some bannock, lard and butter, jam and an open can of corned beef. "Get up, partner," I called, "coffee is ready." Jumbie, a great sport and fine man on the trail, peeped out from under his blankets, mumbled something about daylight and crazy white men who put more trust in their watch than in the good Lord's old sun.

At breakfast I said: "We are out of fresh meat, we will have to eat horse meat; here, have some, it is not bad when we are hungry!" — "No thanks," he said, not too pleased with our frugal menu of bannock, butter and at any rate he preferred lard to butter and jam. — "Won't you have some meat?" I asked again, "we may have a long day." He shook his head. "What is the matter now? are you sick or just not hungry?" — "No," he said, me no eat horse meat." — "Oh! oh! I got you this time, it is corned beef, eat!" We shared our breakfast on this joyous note.

The goal of the day was to reach Fontas. Rushing his last cup of coffee, Jumbie disappeared on his large trail breaking snowshoes; he would go as far as Eddy Needlay's trail and return to meet me. I loaded the toboggans, a lighter load in front for Jumbie's small dogs and the remainder of the outfit for mine. Jumbie's wide snowshoes were barely marking the trail; with my trail snowshoes, I could sink about five to seven inches but, in the spring granulated snow the dogs could not reach a solid footing. The only way we could advance was for me to walk ahead for some distance, to track back and to push the first load while urging my dogs to follow . . . Mush! Mush! at a very slow pace to the point already broken and then to repeat the operation again and again. By 10:30 a.m. Jumbie's dogs were not anxious to go any more despite the rest period my little trip ahead and back would grant them.

We were not going anywhere that way, I had to think of something else. I put ten dogs on one toboggan with my old Mike on the lead; it was easier but, I would have to come back to get the other load. On and on, we huffed and puffed like this until 4 p.m. There was no sign of Jumbie coming back, I knew then that he had not come across Needlay's fresh trail; all hope of reaching Fontas by night had vanished. I made a tea camp but, while the water was boiling, I extended it to an overnight camp.

I downed a few cups of tea, chewed a piece of dried meat and snowshoed back four to five miles to fetch the other toboggan; even without pulling a load, it was hard going for the dogs. I do not remember all the details of this return trip except that there was much pushing and sweating, shouting and urging and before long it was complete darkness. It was about 10:30 p.m. when I first saw the glow of the camp. Jumbie had great fire going, had prepared supper, cooked dog food, and the tea pail was steaming. "Come," he said, "have a good cup of tea, Eat." "I will tie up the dogs." He had already made spruce bough beds for them. I stood near the fire to dry up a bit but soon dipped in the tea pail for a mighty cup.

"How far did you go, seen any trail?" — "I stopped on top of the Sikanni hill; no sign of anybody, just wonder what happened to Eddy?" — "We shall see tomorrow, I guess." "Eat" insisted Jumbie. "I think I should just forget about it and hit the sack! I will need no rocking either. It has been a long day, certainly the longest of my life. From 4:30 a.m. to 11 p.m. is a long shift indeed."

A cool north wind whirled some smoke around our head, the stars were slightly veiled with a thin ice fog but, the northern lights were very busy swishing and switching in the northwest. We got up late in the chilly morning and made it easily to Fontas where we found a group of happy people. The return trip was no problem either; on the frozen trail we could cover in one hour the distance of a long day in the way in.

Since this trip I often thought about snowshoes; without them we would have been prisoners of the elements. To understand their value, one must know about snow and crippling power; it takes a sudden and heavy snowfall to remind modern cities dwellers of the entrapping reality of these otherwise enjoyable flakes. The early people of the north who had to face the bare facts of long winters came up with a triumpant answer, the snowshoes. Few days ago during a heavy snowstorm, a young lad was joyfully wandering around on snowshoes; had he tried to walk without them, he would have disappeared in the powdery stuff. Snowshoes are still a vital instrument of survival in our northern winters. Travelling with dogteams, snowshoes are either

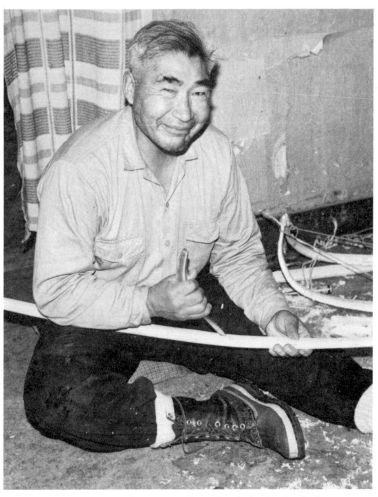

Handcrafted snowshoes, a trademark of the Teslin Indians.

used or carefully tied up on top of the load near the gun. Many experienced northerners do not discard their snowshoes while switching to more modern ways of transportation they are found behind snowmobiles; bush pilots rate them high among other survival gears.

Our native people are still using snowshoes extensively and fortunately have preserved the art of making them. Teslin Tlingit Indians have inherited the typical shoes which reflect the experi-

Paul Jackson and Walter Fox drilling holes in snowshoe frames.

ence of many generations of mighty travellers in the white wilderness and of smart trappers and hunters.

Usually the frame is made of birch; the foot rest is strung with heavy raw moosehide strings, the toe and the heel are woven with half tanned caribou hide strips. The result is great! a happy mixture of strength and lightness. Our local craftsmen produce several hundred entirely handmade pairs each year to fill the demand of local customers but also on request from many points of Canada and of the United States as far south as Florida, Texas and New Mexico. Why do people of the south want snowshoes? Not always for practical use indeed, but to possess a famous handicraft; to own a genuine pair of Teslin snowshoes is a treasure in itself! They make a nice decoration over the fireplace or in the amusement room. Teslin snowshoes are like the Stradivarius of the snowshoes, the best solution to a major problem, in short, the overall best, in my opinion.

J. P. Tanguay
Teslin, Yukon

The finished snowshoes on display at Teslin, Yukon.

THE WHITE EARTH

Telegraphic code, or Morse code as more commonly known is an internationally recognized code of language. It was invented by Samuel Morse in the 1860's. Strictly speaking, the only parts of the Morse Code which would pertain to a snowshoer in trouble would be the SOS signals. However, if you have a flashlight, or there are abundant rocks or other such things around, you could communicate your needs to the rescue teams looking for you.

International Morse Code

Letters

A	di-dah	**J**	di-dah-dah-dah	**S**	di-di-dit	
B	dah-di-di-dit	**K**	dah-di-dah	**T**	dah	
C	dah-di-dah-dit	**L**	di-dah-di-dit	**U**	di-di-dah	
D	dah-di-dit	**M**	dah-dah	**V**	di-di-di-dah	
E	dit	**N**	dah-dit	**W**	di-dah-dah	
F	di-di-dah-dit	**O**	dah-dah-dah	**X**	dah-di-di-dah	
G	dah-dah-dit	**P**	di-dah-dah-dit	**Y**	dah-di-dah-dah	
H	di-di-di-dit	**Q**	dah-dah-di-dah	**Z**	dah-dah-di-dit	
I	di-dit	**R**	di-dah-dit			

Numerals

1	di-dah-dah-dah-dah	**6**	dah-di-di-di-dit
2	di-di-dah-dah-dah	**7**	dah-dah-di-di-dit
3	di-di-di-dah-dah	**8**	dah-dah-dah-di-dit
4	di-di-di-di-dah	**9**	dah-dah-dah-dah-dit
5	di-di-di-di-dit	**0**	dah-dah-dah-dah-dah

In selecting the right snowshoes for you there are several factors you should take into consideration:

1. Terrain— will it be flat, open, trails, bush?

2. Snow conditions— light powder or deep and crusty.

3. Usage— hunting, back packing, forestry work, or general recreation.

4. Weight and height of the person using the snowshoes.

5. Experience— are you a rookie or a pro?

A young snowshoer reflects on his trip through the woods.

A beautiful vista observed from a pair of snowshoes.